Advance Praise For
Why Lawyers (and the Rest of Us) Lie And Engage In Other Repugnant Behavior
By Mark Perlmutter

In attempting to introduce the principles of community into the practice of law in our ever increasingly adversarial society, Mark Perlmutter is a courageous prophet and a man of healing. His vision is desperately needed.
M. Scott Peck, M.D.,
Best-selling Author of *The Road Less Traveled*

Through fascinating behind-the-scenes stories and unflinching self-revelation, Mark Perlmutter takes us deep into a culture that places persuasion and manipulation far above cooperation and collaboration. Yet this book is not just about the legal profession; it's about the power and possibility of openness and authenticity for all of us, whether in a courtroom, an office building, or our own living rooms.
Dave Potter, President 3D, Inc.,
organizational consulting, Moscow, Idaho

... for those persons who are genuinely concerned about the profession and the way it often acts, this book can be a valuable contribution if not prescription.
Sherman Cohn, Prof. of Law, Georgetown Univ.;
Former Pres., American Inns of Court

I greatly enjoyed *Why Lawyers Lie* ... I fully embrace [the] view that the need for cooperative behavior, based on trust, is a superior alternative to win-lose adversarial relationships.
Mark G. Yudof, Former Dean, University of Texas Law School; Pres. of the University of Minnesota

WHY
LAWYERS

(AND THE REST OF US)

LIE

**AND
ENGAGE IN
OTHER REPUGNANT
BEHAVIOR**

by Mark Perlmutter

BRIGHT

BOOKS

Library of Congress Catalog Number: 98-70906

ISBN 1-880092-47-6

First Edition

12 11 10 9 8 7 6 5 4 3 2 1

Bright Books
P.O. Box 50335
Austin, Texas 78763-0335
512-499-4164
Fax 512-477-9975

To

Eric & Lindsay

CONTENTS

ACKNOWLEDGMENTS

I would like to acknowledge . . .

My parents for the gift of life and so much more.

My children, Eric and Lindsay, for their love, and for making me very proud.

My life partner, Alexis, for her special gifts and continuing surprises.

My brother, Bill, for the way he serves.

My mentors who have helped me to find the best within myself: Yvonne Agazarian, Roger Armstrong, Lloyd Doggett, Judge Royal Furgeson, Rabbi Steven Folberg, Kaz Gozdz, Roger Hall, June Gallessich, Ann Hoewing, Larry Hope, Diane Ireson, Tommy Jacks, Nelson Marks, Mary K. Marsden, Bill McCarley, Scotty Peck (who can count me among the millions whom he has profoundly affected), Jack Ratliff, Beverly Reeves, Bob Reiff, Bob Roberts, Blair Singer, Jev and Sydnor Sikes, John Sutton, Clara Walmsley, and Tom Watkins.

My law firm, for keeping my life in order throughout this process—Sherry Aalbu, Jared Caplan, Amy Crane, Bertha Endsley, Elizabeth Geller, Jennifer Martin, Maricela Koopman, Jennifer Gabel Perez, Loriann Priour, Michael Roseberry, Brooks Schuelke, Monique Terrell, Elizabeth Woodhead, and Jana Visser.

My extraordinary office manager, Sherry Aalbu, who has striven tirelessly for perfection.

My able staff members—Jared Caplan, Amy Crane, Jennifer Martin, and Jennifer Gabel Perez—who provided invaluable help in dealing with the pesky details of word-processing and cite-checking.

Researchers Ron Alves, Cecile Foy, Jennifer Martin, Kristi Pruett, and Elizabeth Woodhead.

My law partner, Brad Rock Reagan, for his abiding friendship and support during my many forays outside of the world of the law.

Bert Pluymen, for his practical guidance, encouragement, and spirit.

Those whose insights, edits, suggestions, and encouragement enlivened the spirit of the book: Marianne Baker, Lisa Barnett, Martha Boston, Bob Frachtman, Ann Hoewing, Neil Iscoe, Adrienne Kennedy, Martha Kipcak, Cynthia Lee, Lynne Liberato, Jennifer Gabel Perez, Justice Tom Phillips, Ronnie Raben, Jack Ratliff, Justice Tom Reavley, Sydnor Sikes, John Sutton, Brian Turner, Paul Van Osselaer, and Betsy Whitaker—particularly for introducing me to new vistas.

Katrina and Andy Bonner for their invaluable cooperation in publishing the advance edition, and John Patterson for his elegantly simple and creative cover design.

My agent, Kathleen Davis Niendorff—without her encouragement and tenacity, I doubt I would've written the book.

My editor and friend, John Trimble, who has enabled me to say what I know so that others may hear it, and has made me a better writer than I (and some of my former teachers) ever thought was possible.

And last, but certainly not least, my clients, who have given me the privilege of their trust and confidence.

INTRODUCTION

Why *do* lawyers lie? Besides being deceptive, why are we also often greedy and hostile? And what is the connection, if any, between our hostility and the litigiousness of Americans in general, who file around 14 million civil lawsuits a year in state courts alone?[1]

I've spent over 20 years as a trial lawyer watching people rail against one another in grossly unproductive conflict. Whether it's actually worse than it was 50 years ago, I don't know. People with agendas can cite statistics both ways. I do know, however, from personal experience, not to mention daily reports on the national news, that our differences in this country generate enormously wasteful strife.

Consider the eternal war between the sexes now waged in courthouses nationwide. Before the '70s, victims of sexual harassment had no legal remedy. Yet the advent of a remedy does not seem to have deterred this type of cliched behavior, the subject of a classic sexual-harassment lawsuit:

Summoned by a man of influence, she approached their meeting place with some apprehension and tentatively knocked on the door.

He opened it, greeted her with a smile, and shook her hand, then led her into a room comfortably furnished with a couch, reading lamps, and chairs.

As the door closed behind her, he offered small talk. *"How are things going at work?"*

"Fine," she began, *"but, you know, some days are better than others."*

"Yeah, I've been thinking about that. In fact, I dreamt I got you a promotion and you were so grateful, you did me a favor in return."

---

[1] About 16 million civil lawsuits were filed in state courts in 1988 (White 203-204). Between 1992 and 1994, the number dropped from 15.3 million to 14.3 million ("National Criminal Justice Measures" 1).

Naively, she took the bait. *"What kind of favor?"*

He smiled, proffered a lascivious invitation, and calmly awaited her response...

"Oh, God!" she exclaimed to herself. Trapped between satisfying this sexual aggressor or refusing him and probably losing her job, she could only babble: *"I'm sorry. I-I had no idea.... I don't understand. What are you saying?"*

"I think you know what I'm saying," he insisted, slithering toward her.

Terrified, she bolted out the door. The following week she lost her job.

Although these facts are similar, they are not the basis of the now-famous case of *Paula Corbin Jones v. William Jefferson Clinton*.[2] Unlike *Jones v. Clinton*, this case settled quickly for a fair sum and without undue litigation costs. In contrast, *Jones v. Clinton* has generated a national spectacle.

While some might think that sexual-harassment cases are frivolous by their nature, I don't. When employees lose job opportunities for rebuffing sexual advances, or when employers subject them to recurring unwelcome advances sufficient to creates a hostile work environment, the legal system should and does provide redress. All too often, the evil addressed by sexual-harassment laws is real.

Nevertheless, in many cases, I find myself thinking, "What a waste!" Where do sexual aggressors check their brains? Surely, long before getting sued, they have been given feedback that their seduction technique is not only wanting but offensive. And in some cases, isn't there some way other than a lawsuit to remedy the problem? How many lost hours, how many dollars, and how much aggravation and heartache may come out of a bumbling, impotent pass?

---

[2] In her pleadings, Jones alleged that while Governor of Arkansas, Clinton had a state trooper bring her to a hotel room where Clinton first discussed her job and then made sexual overtures which she refused. Jones later alleged that Clinton used his influence to hamper her career.

And while we're discussing wasteful conflict, here's another example, this one captured in a report by one of my legal assistants summarizing a phone conversation she'd had with a potential client:

On Saturday, November 11, 1996, Tony, a black man, entered a [Bigoil] convenience store to buy a beer. The white clerk asked him to show his I.D., whereupon he flashed his military I.D. card. The clerk said she could not accept his military I.D. and asked him for his driver's license. Tony then showed his out-of-state license. The clerk said she could not take anything but a Texas I.D.

Tony went to the car and asked his wife to come in and show her Texas driver's license. She did so, and the clerk began ringing up the beer. Tony's wife then said to him within earshot of the clerk, "See, I didn't want to stop at [Bigoil]." (Although she didn't say so, Tony knew that her objection to stopping was because of Bigoil's reputation as a discriminatory company.) Apparently offended by the wife's remark, the clerk told Tony and his wife that she was refusing service because they were showing her improper I.D. They said they HAD shown her proper I.D. The clerk wrote a note that said, "Service refused—improper I.D. [Signed,] Melba." She then handed it to the wife. The wife began arguing with the clerk, whereupon the clerk threatened to "call the cops." They said, "Fine, call the cops." So the clerk called the police and complained that Tony's wife's language and attitude were causing problems. The police agreed to come, and Tony and his wife stayed until they arrived.

After hearing the clerk's complaints of foul and rude language, and Tony and his wife's complaint that the clerk had improperly refused service, the policeman said that he did not know of any law that prohibited the purchase of liquor without a Texas driver's license. Otherwise, the policeman said he couldn't do anything—that "it was a civil matter."

Tony and his wife were embarrassed and humiliated. They want to know if there is any legal recourse.

Although some would see this matter as "just another frivolous lawsuit," I don't. Legally, it was not at all frivolous. The law prohibits discrimination in public accommodations; Tony and his wife may indeed have been refused service on account of race. Still, I once again find myself thinking, "What a waste!" What is the cost in hours, dollars, aggravation, and humiliation that may come out of one moment of possibly race-based rudeness? And what about the untold thousands of other instances of senseless conflict? How many once-happy marriages end in divorce? How many divorces consume every dollar of financial and emotional capital that a family has? How many business ventures and construction projects degenerate into protracted litigation? How many insurance claims unnecessarily end up in the courthouse?

The failure to handle conflict productively exacts a fortune in "transaction costs"—the costs of getting the matter settled. And these of course come right out of the combatants' own pockets. Take, for instance, the huge lawsuit between a certain chemical company and its insurer that I'll be discussing further in Chapter 12. The law firms involved billed *tens of millions of dollars* in legal fees and case expenses. Retrospectively, lawyers from both sides acknowledge that the lawsuit could have been prevented—or at the very least shortened. What a waste!

As an attorney, I know conflict. Few people experience more conflict in everyday life than trial lawyers. My clients usually have but one lawsuit going, whereas I might be representing, at any given time, up to 50 clients in as many lawsuits. Day-in and day-out, for well more than eight hours a day, my *job* is dealing with conflict. And when it is unproductive, as it often is, it is painful for all concerned, including me. What a waste!

In sexual-harassment cases, in interracial conflict, in the chemical-company case, and indeed in every failed relationship, distancing others unnecessarily provokes and prolongs the conflict. For example, in the chemical-company case, the insurance company elected to stonewall the chemical company. Had it chosen instead to be conciliatory, vast sums in legal fees probably would have been saved. Similarly, in the convenience-store encounter, had the cashier been cooperative with her customers, or had the customers been willing to cut the cashier some slack like you would a kid who just didn't know any better,[3] a wasteful police call and possible lawsuit could have been averted. In sexual-harassment cases, if the perpetrators would recognize that their sometimes clumsy, sometimes vicious advances only alienate their objects of desire and predictably generate strife for themselves, far fewer suits would arise. And on the other hand, if those who might be harassed were able to set clear boundaries without unnecessarily further provoking their pursuer,[4] both the chances of repeated advances or retaliation for spurning them would be reduced. In turn, many employee grievances and even lawsuits might be averted.

In truth, the choices that people make to distance themselves from one another are at the root of all unproductive conflict. Instead of choosing to say and do things to alleviate the friction between them, they choose to aggravate the conflict. The kind of distance that results bears the seeds of every lawsuit that's filed.

From boardroom to boudoir, most of us[5] handle conflict in a way that only increases the distance between ourselves and others. As we repeatedly experience such results, we begin to expect them. Assuming it's "dog-eat-dog," we resolve to eat before we're eaten—and so continue a vicious cycle of deception and hostility.

---

[3] Given the history of vicious racial discrimination in America, admittedly, such forbearance is a lot to expect.

[4] I'm not suggesting that such equanimity is appropriate in cases of continuous pursuit or those involving invasive physical touching. And the power imbalances that invariably exist in sexual harassment cases are likely to rattle even the coolest composure.

[5] There are times in this book when I include myself among my audience. I may say, for example, "We are often unconscious of how our actions affect others." While my intent is to include myself as one who is often unconscious of how my actions affect others, and while I have personally seen others who are also similarly unconscious, I do not presume that everyone reading this book is also unconscious. Thus, when I say "we," I mean "those of us for whom this is an issue."

Unproductive conflict occurs not only in lawsuits but in virtually every aspect of American life. Consider the popularity of bashing. Instead of looking for ways to ameliorate conflict, we habitually attack one another. Republicans bash Democrats; Democrats bash Republicans; we all bash our federal bureaucracy. Siblings bash siblings; spouses bash spouses; we all bash our parents. Law enforcement bashes suspected criminals; suspected criminals bash law enforcement; and they all bash our courts. Environmentalists bash industry; industry bashes environmentalists; and they all bash the regulators. Insurance companies bash trial lawyers; trial lawyers bash insurance companies; and we all bash the legislature. (And, naturally, *everybody* bashes lawyers!) Psychologist Yvonne Agazarian says that when we have feelings so strong that we literally can't contain them, we find an external target for them— and bash it. But of course our bashing engenders still more fear and mistrust, driving us ever further apart.

Where is the answer? I find a promising lead in John F. Kennedy's *Profiles in Courage.* One story that Kennedy tells is that of Mississippi Senator Lucius Lamar (133-153). Himself known before the Civil War as "one of the most rabid 'fire-eaters' to come out of the deep South" (134), Lamar, by a curious turn of fate, delivered a post-war eulogy to a man whom Kennedy called "the South's most implacable enemy" (133), Senator Charles Sumner of Massachusetts. At a time when each side still despised the other, Lamar concluded his eulogy with these healing words:

> Would that the spirit of the illustrious dead whom we lament today could speak from the grave to both parties to this deplorable discord in tones which should reach each and every heart throughout this broad territory: "My countrymen! know one another, and you will love one another!" (134)

Kennedy continues:

> There was an ominous silence.... Then a spontaneous burst of applause rolled out from all sides.

"My God, what a speech!" said Congressman Lyman Tremaine of New York.... "It will ring through the country." ....[Lamar's speech] marked a turning point in relations between the North and South. (134)

In that exquisite instant, Lamar had conveyed that the North no longer need fear the formerly rebellious South, and expressed a fervent desire by the South to rekindle the spirit of national community. Before Senator Lamar spoke, many northern Senators had wanted to continue to subjugate the South under military rule. But Lamar's speech triggered the end of the North's domination of the South, and began a period of cooperation toward the mutual well-being of the two regions.

Time after time, Kennedy honors a particular kind of courage, namely, the courage of individuals choosing to overcome personal obstacles in order to bring divided Americans together. In the case of Senator Lamar, the personal obstacles included not only his long hatred of the North, but also the risk of being perceived by other southerners as a turncoat.

What if Republicans and Democrats similarly had the courage to heal the wounds between them?

Another statesman to whom Kennedy pays tribute is Daniel Webster, whom Kennedy calls "the most talented figure in congressional history" (56). Why did Webster rate such exalted praise? Because, Kennedy says, he had the "ability to make alive and supreme the latent sense of oneness, of union, that all Americans felt but which few could express" (56). In hindsight, Kennedy may have overrated Webster, but what's significant here is what Kennedy values as supreme—building a sense of American community.

Another Kennedy hero, Senator Sam Houston, is profiled for his efforts to preserve the Union even though it placed him at odds with his Texas constituency, which favored slavery and secession (89-106). Thomas Hart Benton was yet another who broke loyalties for the sake of the union—and thereby guaranteed his political defeat (72-88). Both of them, too, were men of courage, Kennedy says.

Though Kennedy celebrates only the courage of storied legislators, it is equally possible for the rest of us to exhibit similar courage in dealing with everyday conflicts. Consider the common workplace occurrence of a boss being dissatisfied with an employee's performance. The boss may react so that he or she places obstacles in the way of a positive working relationship, perhaps by exploding in anger ("Dammit! How many times have I told you that when we set a deadline, I expect it to be kept!") or by being silently resentful. On a better day, though, the boss might find the courage to risk dislike by factually identifying the problem ("I noticed that you missed our deadline yesterday"). The boss may then be willing to give up controlling with anger by enlisting the employee's help in preventing the problem from recurring ("How can we work together to keep that from happening again?")—a result that will bring the two of them closer together. Even if the boss momentarily loses his temper, the relationship can be repaired by his apologizing for his outburst and respectfully engaging the employee in problem-solving.

Every human conflict is finally a test of our courage. The choice is invariably the same: we can continue trying to resolve conflict in ways that ultimately drive us further apart, which in turn increases the strife of daily living and rends the fabric of our society, or we can use conflict as an opportunity to acknowledge and deal with our own contributions to it and thereby grow closer together. This book aims to explore how each of us can find such courage in conflict.

Our starting point is the American civil-justice system—the place that unproductive conflict calls home. For it is here that our body politic channels the symptoms of our malaise.

When we seek justice from the system that bears its name, what do we encounter? Clients, lawyers, and judges cooperatively engaged in a high-minded pursuit of justice? Hardly—at least not often. Day to day, we find lies and deception, hostility, and greed. These are the stuff of unproductive conflict. In addition to the fact that conflict is concentrated there, another reason to begin our focus on strife within the civil-justice system is that its dynamics mirror how we deal with disputes in our daily lives—in our intimate relationships, with friends, in the workplace, and in and among our private and governmental institutions. Although it may be uncomfortable, many of us may see in the stories about legal clashes some ways in which we ourselves fail to effectively resolve daily disagreements.

Let me give a brief overview of what lies ahead. The first five chapters address the question of why lawyers—and, in fact, most other people—engage in lying and other repugnant behavior. Chapter 1 focuses on the lying. Chapters 2–4 deal with the hostility pandemic in our civil-justice system. Chapter 5, meanwhile, examines behavior motivated by greed. Chapter 6 then explores some proposed solutions to such behavior and explains their inadequacy. Chapter 7 reveals how the intolerability of our behavior, even given the current attempts at solutions, portends revolutionary change.

Then, in Part II, we'll look at conflict in context. We'll explore factors that we don't even normally think about and see how they provide a framework for approaching conflict in a new and genuinely powerful way—a way I call "centered conflict resolution."™

Part III examines that new way in detail.

This is, for me, a very personal book. As I'll reveal throughout, I've had to overcome some demons of my own to write it. That's meant confronting my own lies, my own hostility, and my own greed—not just to find personal peace, but to say something of value here, something that goes beyond the usual platitudes of ethics and professionalism. I confess I have found little value in most others' pontifications on those subjects. And why? Because I don't believe that most of them practice their own preaching. Their answers feel too pat. They exhibit no signs of personal struggle. Before I was willing to acknowledge my own struggle, I was probably guilty of such pontification myself. But I hope that my vulnerability here will inspire courage.

Perhaps the only thing more wasteful than railing against one another in grossly unproductive conflict is

PROLOGUE

The doors were closed and the conversation hushed as three lawyers discussed some notes scribbled on a sheet of legal paper. After they had passed the paper among themselves, one of them crumpled it and tossed it in a wastebasket. There it nestled, indistinguishable from the other discarded paper-balls.

But this one was different. It was evidence.

Arthur[7] had written the notes several years earlier. They were part of his case file that had been subpoenaed in connection with a lawsuit. Several statements in the notes were inconsistent with the sworn testimony that Arthur was about to give at a deposition in the next room.

John, the second member of the trio, was "preparing" Arthur for his deposition. Other lawyers esteemed John for both his skill and his ethics. He was, and is, admired by lawyers, judges, and laymen alike. Yet as he threw away the damning sheet of paper, he did so decisively, with no sign of ambivalence. In fact, the decision seemed instinctive.

Until that time, I had hoped someday to be just like John. And that was one of many reasons I stood silently by as a little piece of my soul fell among the crinkled balls of paper in the wastebasket.

---

[7] The names used in this book are fictitious. While I have described events as accurately as memory permits, I have taken some liberties with fact descriptions so as to preserve confidences.

complaining about incivility by railing against *it*.[6] Railing at it is no remedy. The only way we can effectively reduce social strife is by owning up to, and overcoming, our own contributions to it. I aspire here to practice what I preach.

Although Part I focuses on lawyer misbehavior, this book is not about bashing lawyers. Many lawyers work hard and compassionately in the service of their clients, often for little appreciation. At their best, they are honest and generous. But, like everyone else, lawyers have a dark side—and it happens to be a slave to the justice system. By that I mean two things. First, by temperament and training, we lawyers are often eager to embrace the warfare that goes with litigation. And second, even if we aren't so temperamentally inclined, the system often triggers our gladiatorial impulses. I hope this book will inspire lawyers to take responsibility for the impact of our dark sides on the civil-justice system, and to lead—with others weary of destructive conflict—a peaceful revolution over its tyranny.

Why would lawyers want to save others from the rampant strife that generates lawyer livelihoods? Because if the legal profession does not lead the rescue, the legal profession itself will be among its casualties.

---

[6] When I speak of incivility, I don't mean just bad manners. I mean a deeper failing—a lack of consideration of another's humanity.

PART I

WHY LAWYERS
(AND THE REST OF US)
LIE

AND ENGAGE IN
OTHER REPUGNANT
BEHAVIOR

INTRODUCTION
TO PART I

Over the years, I have endured a private shame from my role in the destruction of Arthur's notes. I have also wondered, "Why did I do that? Why did John do that?"

After all, I *am* a respectable lawyer. I've served on the state bar's Professionalism Committee. I make speeches and write papers to educate other trial lawyers. I guest-lecture at a prestigious law school. My colleagues have elected me president of our local Young Lawyers Association and, later, president of our county bar association. I have even served on the board of directors of our state bar association. More ironic still, I helped write the "Texas Lawyers Creed, a Mandate For Professionalism"!

John is respectable, too. In the years since he destroyed Arthur's notes, John has held a statewide bar association office. He has also won recognition from his peers for his accomplishments both as a lawyer and as a legal scholar. A generous, compassionate person, John enjoys an idyllic family life.

So why would John and I, two well-regarded, successful lawyers, risk our careers by doing something patently illegal? Did we share some deep-seated character flaw? Were we victims of temporary insanity? Or was there a more complex explanation?

Although character can never be separated from conduct, I believe that other factors entered in here—factors that touch the lives of virtually all of us.

It is tempting, however, to look at the events described in the prologue in isolation: just three lawyers in a room by themselves conspiring to destroy evidence, their actions the result of individual decisions by individual people. This temptation to say, "It's just her nature" or "He's just a jerk," is deeply ingrained in our culture, particularly in lawyers,[8] perhaps the leading experts in laying blame on individual character—so long as it's someone else's.

Americans like things short and simple, especially when fixing blame. We lawyers know this principle well. We use it all the time to manipulate juries. Consider the case of a man working at a fast-food chain who's assaulted by a fellow employee high on drugs. The motive is robbery. The method is a brain-spattering blow to the head with a dough hook and then suffocation induced by a plastic bag tied around the neck. The victim's survivors sue the fast-food chain because the robber has no money. What makes it all the food chain's fault? A short, simple phrase: "This is a lax-security case." Never mind that the murderer had a depraved family life. Never mind that he had been to prison and not been treated for drug abuse there. Never mind that the educational system may have failed him. Never mind that television displays similar occurrences on more channels than one could possibly watch. Never mind that violence in America has reached epidemic proportions. Never mind that multiple causes explain such events. Lawyers know that jurors just want to know who's to blame. Calling it a "lax-security case" finds a single villain—the fast-food chain.

Politicians also know the magic of keeping it short and simple. Sound bites, 30-second commercials, character assassinations—all these pander to the same fixation: tell us who's to blame, who's right and who's wrong, and be quick about it. Most of us don't want to take the time or energy to analyze the complexities surrounding the issues of the day—crime, health care, race relations, international politics, or whatever. Witness the instant (though short-lived) appeal of Ross Perot's flip charts and "It's just that simple" approach in the 1992 Presidential campaign.

---

[8] In a self-described "National Monthly For Litigators and Litigation Managers," six California lawyers participated in a roundtable discussion in which one decried the rising number of "bad apples" in the profession. ("Separating the Just" 24-29). Moreover, the very title of the article, "Separating the Just from the Jerks," reflects the tendency among lawyers to place the blame for bad behavior on individual character.

But if our society resists complexity in most other contexts, why would we embrace it when discussing such an easy target as lawyers? Ordinarily, we wouldn't. But if we are to find meaningful solutions to unproductive conflict, we must be willing to open our eyes to the truth, even if it is complex and uncomfortable.

The truth is, everyone has the capacity to be destructive as well as virtuous. And, although some people are consistently more able than others to control their dark sides (Graziano, Jensen-Campbell and Hair 820), situational factors powerfully affect our inclination toward destructive behavior (Zimbardo 4:155-170).

Do you recall the famous psychology experiment on obedience to authority conducted at Yale University back in the '50s? The subjects, chosen from the ranks of Yale students, local businessmen, and ordinary citizens of Bridgeport, Connecticut, were told that, as part of a learning experiment, they were to administer an increasingly stronger electric shock to a person each time the person made a mistake on a test. The lever on the purported electrical device went clear up to 450 volts. The subjects could hear the "learners" over an intercom but not see them. Although the "learners" were not really shocked, they were told to cry out and mention having heart problems as the voltage increased. If a subject ever hesitated to administer the shock, he or she was sternly told that the experiment *required* the administering of electric shocks. Over 60% of the subjects eventually administered *the full 450 volts!*

In corporate settings, too, situational factors have been viewed as significant determinants of behavior. W. Edwards Deming, the man credited with engineering Japan's postwar dominance in world commerce, estimates that only 6% of what goes wrong in a system is attributable to an individual person or thing; the rest stems from other factors (Mixon and Otto 393, 399). For example, if a person's eligibility for a pay raise rests solely on maximizing the number of widgets she produces, she has a disincentive to ensure quality, even though she may personally believe in it.

From repeated experiences with one another, we lawyers know that we're all capable of cussedness. It may

or may not emerge, we've learned, depending on our circumstances. For example, we may be hostile only when
other lawyers are hostile. Or we may be unethical only
when having to choose between competing loyalties, such
as loyalty to our clients versus loyalty to the judicial system.

But the American tendency to oversimplify and blame
casts lawyers invariably as cussed. This tendency to scape-
goat lawyers is not only simplistic but it also masks the
more complex causes of unproductive conflict. To find the
path to courage, we must understand our current behavior
in all its complexity, including external factors that bring
out the worst in all of us.

Finding the path to courage also requires an accurate
and honest assessment of our actions. How, after all, can
we even begin to understand our behavior unless we first
acknowledge it? In Part I, I acknowledge my own lying
and other repugnant behavior—as an individual and as a
member of the legal profession—while I explore the factors that bring out the worst in all of us.

CHAPTER 1

LIES AND DECEPTION

*In any swearing match, at least half the people are
lying—and that's not even counting the lawyers.*

With outright lies and forged documents, Austin bankruptcy lawyer Debra Bates defrauded her client Dave
Roberts and his family out of $228,000 over a six-month
period in the early '90s. Ensuing legal proceedings against
Bates uncovered thefts of over a million dollars from other
clients who, like Mr. Roberts, had put their trust in her.
Within the year, after being vigorously pursued in civil
suits, criminal investigations, and disbarment proceedings,
Debra Bates committed suicide.

Fortunately, the Bates debacle was a rare case of egre-
gious dishonesty. But what's truly pernicious in the American legal system is the daily dissembling about which
most of us are unconscious. Just as the Exxon Valdez disas-
ter, bad as it was, pales alongside the toxic effect of millions of everyday emissions, the Bates case is nothing next
to the everyday noxious duplicities in our civil-justice system. This chapter identifies the nature and causes of such
lies and deception.

I'll begin with a story of how we lawyers trap our
opponents by our own concealment of information.

Perched on the stand like a parrot on a bar, the witness's barrel-chested body was so noticeably top-heavy
that I wondered how he was able to remain upright.

His pulpy face had skin the texture of ladies' glove leather. His arrow-straight hair glistened with oil. He had a certain polyester presence.

"State your name for the record."
"Billy Bob Potts."
"Were you once married to Sally Potts?"
"Yeah."
"Do you understand that she has accused you of physically abusing her?"
"Yeah, that's what she says."
"Do you deny that on May 17, 1976, you grabbed her by the throat and rammed her head up against the doorsill?"
"Yeah, I deny it."
"You are certain that you never grabbed her by the throat and rammed her head up against the doorsill?"
"Yeah."
"I'm handing you what has been marked as Plaintiff's Exhibit 1. Do you recognize the handwriting?"
"Yeah."
"Whose is it?"
"It's mine."
"What is this notebook that has your writing in it?"
"It's my diary."
"What's the date on the top of this page right here."
"May 17, 1976."

Even at this point, the Parrot shows no recognition that he has already toppled from his perch and is plunging toward a head-first landing.

"Will you please read what you have written on this page in your diary?"
"'I grabbed Sally by the throat and rammed her head up against the doorsill'."

How We Deceive and Justify It

Litigation is a paradox: it will often seek the truth through artful deception. Sometimes that deception takes the form of concealment, as was convenient here to expose Mr. Potts as a wife-beater. He was deceived, first, by his wife's covert snatching of his diary, and then by my concealing my possession of it until he had committed himself to his lie.

In *Potts v. Potts*, the concealment may not have been essential to exposing the truth, but it certainly simplified the task. Mr. Potts had not reached what I call the "plausible-lie threshold"—that is, he did not yet possess sufficient information to enable him to concoct a plausible lie. His outright denial that he did not "ram her head against the doorsill" was not a plausible lie in light of the revelation of his admission in his diary. On the other hand, had Mr. Potts known before testifying that the diary was in his wife's hands, he might have admitted to the act itself and concocted a story that he acted in self-defense against a fabricated assault by his wife. In this way, the knowledge that the diary was in his wife's hands and his refreshed recollection of its contents would have enabled Mr. Potts to reach the plausible-lie threshold.

Lawyers often manage information in lawsuits to prevent opponents from achieving that lie threshold. Whether it is a videotape of the alleged "whiplash" victim performing vigorous exercise, the love letters of a wayward spouse in a divorce case, or a recording of executives conspiring to fix prices, the impact of such evidence is always greater if it is disclosed after the opponent has already lied under oath.

Our perception, often rightfully held, is that the other side is lying. In "swearing matches"—lawsuits that hinge solely on credibility—the parties tell stories so contradictory that they cannot possibly both be true. In fact, sometimes *both* parties will lie to bolster their positions. Thus, in any swearing match, at least half the people *are* lying—and that's not even counting the lawyers. Such a perception may be a justification for both legitimate tactics and, as this chapter later explains, those that we consider unethical.

Although I believe the trap for Mr. Potts was ethical, nevertheless, as with all cases of deception, there is a victim, albeit a deserving one. When we lawyers victimize people, even deserving ones, we reinforce the perception that the world is a hostile or untrustworthy place. Having been set up by a lawyer, Mr. Potts will hereafter see lawyers as tricky and deceptive. Having also been set up by his ex-wife, he may be less likely to allow others to get close to him.

We pay a similar price because of the way we handle the attorney-client privilege. Lawyers know that we virtually never disclose to the other side all that our clients tell us. For example, an injured plaintiff who claims to have fallen on a slippery ramp may tell his lawyer that he knew to be careful because he'd seen others slip on the ramp before falling himself. On the other hand, the defendant may admit to his lawyer that he himself had fallen on the alleged dangerous ramp the week before the plaintiff fell. Both lawyers are obligated to keep their clients' admissions confidential. Each lawyer may even posture about the strengths of his case during pre-trial settlement negotiations without so much as a whisper of these secret weaknesses. Because each side *knows* the other is hiding at least some information, even legitimately, we distrust one another. And when any of us are suspicious and distant from one another, differences are increasingly likely to fester into conflict. In Part II, we'll look at an alternative.

Until now, we have been discussing deceptive concealment. Let's now consider some situations in which lawyers make affirmative statements that they know are not true— i.e., Lies, with a capital "L."

Perhaps nowhere do lawyers lie more often than in negotiating settlements. Take, for example, cases involving personal injuries. Insurance-company lawyers, acting for defendants in such cases, are often given authority to settle cases by paying a certain amount—say, $100,000. Typically, then, they'll begin negotiations by telling the opposing counsel, "All I've got is $75,000." Plaintiffs' lawyers, meanwhile, are often given authority by their clients to settle the case for "whatever you think is best." So, in our example case, the plaintiff's lawyer will usually counter, "My client will not agree to take that amount."

Such lies are in fact the norm in settlement discussions. In fact, one well-known lawyer friend of mine jokes that "God forgives all lies told in settlement negotiations." And the lying escalates quickly. There are virtually no limits to the creativity that lawyers employ in devising and rationalizing effective lies in such circumstances. For example, lawyers have admitted to me that they've claimed witnesses will say certain favorable things when the witnesses haven't even been contacted. (This practice, in the trade, is called "puffing your case.") Lawyers have also admitted to bluffing that unless someone pays a certain sum of money, they'll sue them. Lawyers are particularly inventive in contriving reasons for why their clients will not accept settlement offers. Typical excuses are "I can't help it. My client's just crazy," and "My client's going to need to get enough money out of this settlement to pay for a tummy-tuck." The fact that these lies are plausible makes them particularly effective.

Many prominent lawyers—whether on the plaintiff side or the defendant side—candidly admit to inventing such ruses. "And why not?" they say. "Everyone knows that's how the game is played."

Another situation in which we lawyers commonly lie is when we're explaining to the judge our need to delay going to trial. The reasons are offered in open court, usually a few days before the trial date. Often the reasons given are bogus. Why? Because the real reasons are not proper grounds for delay. Sometimes, in fact, lawyers will be covering their own embarrassing mistake. So, for example, the lawyer will blithely say,

> "Your honor, the reason we want a continuance [delay] is that my client's uncle is in the hospital and he needs to go be with his aunt."

The truth is, this client couldn't care less about his uncle. The lawyer needs the continuance because he inadvertently omitted the address of a key witness in a pre-trial filing. The lawyer won't be allowed to call that witness to testify unless the trial is delayed, giving the lawyer a chance to correct the oversight. If you happen to sit in on one of these continuance hearings you'll immediately detect when lies are being floated by the knowing smirks of the lawyers in the back of the courtroom when the opposing lawyer mercilessly counters that the real reason for their seeking the continuance is to compensate for a mistake. These smirks say two things:

1. "We know you're lying because we've all done the same thing."
2. "But with our condescending grins we're pretending that we have never made such a bonehead mistake ourselves."

The justification that we lawyers make for such lies resembles the one we give for many of the misleading statements we make in open court: "Well, there is *some* truth to the statement." In short, it's a plausible lie. Everyone knows the real reason for seeking the continuance is to compensate for a mistake, but since a case can be made for another reason, it's the lawyer's job to argue it. After all, that's just part of being an advocate, isn't it? So it really isn't a lie at all.

And it's especially easy to rationalize when the lawyer has blurred the truth with evasive language. Instead of claiming, "This is the reason we want the continuance," we lawyers will argue, "The basis for the continuance is...." That second claim, though misleading, is truthful. It makes no claim about the real reason the continuance is sought. It merely says that this is the basis being offered to justify a proposed result.

Some lawyers, as well as their clients, will actually destroy documents, as did my friend John (with my acquiescence). Kurt Eichenwald of the *New York Times* reported this now infamous scandal:

> Senior executives with Texaco Inc. bantered comfortably among themselves in August 1994, planning the destruction of documents demanded in a federal discrimination lawsuit and describing the company's minority employees with racial epithets.
>
> Unknown to almost everyone in the room, one executive was tape-recording the discussion. (1)

Follow-up stories suggested that the only thing unusual about the Texaco executives' decision was that it was recorded on tape.

Lawyers, if asked, will lie about the existence of documents until it suits their clients' needs. A well-known Houston criminal defense lawyer once told investigators that his client had no documents relevant to their criminal investigation, when in fact the lawyer himself had the documents under lock and key in his own storage facility. When the investigators suggested, much later, that the clients might receive leniency in exchange for cooperation, the documents miraculously appeared. Similar immaculate re-creations of documents occur in civil cases as well.

Another technique for hiding smoking-gun documents is to claim that they are covered by a privilege, such as the one protecting communications between attorneys and their clients. California lawyer Joseph W. Cotchett tells of a friend who called and asked for advice on what the friend perceived to be an ethical dilemma ("Separating the Just" 25). It seems the friend's daughter, a young lawyer working for a Los Angeles law firm, discovered a document in her client's files that would have "explode[d] the litigation." She took the document to her senior partner and asked what to do with it. The senior partner replied: "That's very simple. You just stamp it 'attorney-client privilege' and put it on the privilege log. At the bottom, put down a yellow sticker that says, 'This was reviewed by counsel at the time it was seen.'" The "privilege log" is a list of documents that the other side wants to see but which, because of a claimed privilege, will be kept secret unless a judge orders disclosure after an "in camera" (in private) review. So, in effect, the senior partner was asking the young lawyer to falsify a document to make it appear (to a reviewing judge, if it ever came to that) as if the document was protected from disclosure by the attorney-client privilege. Cotchett chastised the friend, himself a lawyer, for even asking for advice in such a clear-cut case. The friend never called back.

How do we justify lying about the existence or contents of documentary evidence in such circumstances?

Simple: "The other side would do the same." Lying levels the playing field.

In divorce cases, clients, assisted by their lawyers, often lie about the existence of extra-marital affairs. The justification? "We don't want to unnecessarily hurt the other spouse's feelings."

To recap, lawyers commonly cite six justifications for deception:

- It helps expose the truth.
- It helps preserve confidentiality.
- It helps level the playing field.
- It helps achieve a fair result.
- It is harmless because "everyone knows it's done."
- It helps protect the feelings of others.

My purpose here is not to judge the propriety of these "justifications," but only to note that lies and deception are inherently accompanied by them. Whether our justifications hold water or not, that we *are* justifying is, in itself, indicative of a defensive posture. As we'll see in Part II, as long as we're defensively justifying, unproductive conflict thrives.

Sadly, justifications for lying abound inside and outside of the law. In her book *Lying*, Sisela Bok makes a powerful case that our society is pervaded by lies and justifications for them:

> In law and in journalism, in government and in the social sciences, deception is taken for granted when it is felt to be excusable by those who tell the lies and who tend also to make the rules. Government officials and those who run for elections often deceive when they can get away with it and when they assume that the true state of affairs is beyond the comprehension of citizens. Social scientists condone deceptive experimentation on the ground that the knowledge gained will be worth having. Lawyers manipulate the truth in court on behalf of their clients. Those in selling, advertising, or any form of advocacy may mislead the public and their competitors in order to achieve their

goal. Psychiatrists may distort information about their former patients to preserve confidentiality or to keep them out of military service. And journalists, police investigators, and so-called intelligence operators often have little compunction in using falsehoods to gain knowledge they seek. (xvii)

Societally, we show scant awareness of our imperfect integrity. While professing to abhor lying and deceit, we practice them with abandon. That, at least, is the conclusion drawn by James Patterson and Peter Kim, two advertising executives who surveyed over 2,000 Americans as to their habits of lying:

> Americans lie. They lie more than we had ever thought possible before the study. But they told us the truth about how much they lie.
> Just about everyone lies—91 percent of us lie regularly.
> The majority of us find it hard to get through a week without lying. One in five can't make it through a single day—and we're talking about conscious, premeditated lies (Patterson and Kim 45-51).

Another recent survey, this one involving almost 9,000 Americans, ages 15 to 30, by the Joseph and Edna Josephson Institute of Ethics, produced similarly disturbing results:

> More than one-third of all high school and college students said they would lie on a resumé or job application to get a job.... Thirty-nine percent of the college students said they lied to their boss, and 35 percent said they lied to a customer within the past year. (68)

So when lawyers lie, we clearly have a lot of company. All of us, it seems, tend to lie—and to justify it.

The Fear That Drives Deception

Curiously, the details are always scant. I'm sitting in a bunker cut into hard ground, peering over sandbags across a small open field into a dark forest. I'm silently

*firing the weapon on my shoulder, fending off an
unseen enemy. Suddenly, and without warning, my
weapon jams. As I furiously try to fix it, faceless green-
clad soldiers emerge from the forest to overrun my position. With my heart racing in anticipation of certain
death, I awaken in a cold sweat.*

As a young lawyer, I could count on this recurring
nightmare at trial time. It dramatized my deepest fears
about failure and losing. Many times in my career I have
felt like the lone gladiator fighting for survival with imperfect weapons—my wiles, my evidence, and my witnesses.
Sometimes those weapons have misfired, and I have lost.
For many of us, losing at trial feels like a mini-death.[9]

Fear of emotional death is, of course, a powerful impe-
tus for lying. This fear is one reason why many lawyers,
who've gotten along for months during pre-trial discovery,
can be at each other's throats during trial. When survival
is at issue, the anxiety level shoots up, and so does the
temptation to lie.

I recall a trial in the early '80s in which I represented a
nice couple who had bought a house with a faulty slab.
We sued the builder. But during the trial I discovered that
one of my witnesses was going to testify that my clients'
failure to water their grass was part of what caused the slab
to crack. (The dry soil had shrunk.) The witness volunteered to make himself scarce, an offer which I happily
accepted. When I announced in court that I did not
intend to call the witness, the builder's lawyer, guessing
my real motive, called me on it and asked if he was not
correct.[10] I firmly said, "No." I lied because I feared losing.

In addition to that fear, lawyers fear making mistakes and
having them aired in public. Most of us lawyers are over-
achievers who take pride in our self-image of competence.

---

[9] In a survey of about 200 lawyers in the Southeast, 53.4% reported fear of
failing in trial and 62.1% reported worrying "about my practice...in the middle of the night when I should be sleeping." (Papantonio 247-248).

[10] I could have objected to the question, finessing the issue by avoiding an
answer. However, because I feared that such a tactic would have appeared to
the jury to confirm my opponent's suspicions, I opted to lie instead.

Unfortunately, we are in a profession in which someone else has the job—the *job!*—of pointing out those mistakes in the most embarrassing way possible, usually in front of our peers and almost always in public. Hunter S. Thompson, writing in *Rolling Stone*, once made a comment about politics that applies equally to the civil-justice system:

> Politics may be fun, but it's kind of a mean fun— like the rising end of a speed trap or a wide-open hammer shot on some poor son of a bitch who's trapped, and knows it, but can't flee.[11]

Lying is often prompted by the fear of humiliation.

Aside from humiliation, we risk serious economic consequences from making mistakes. Not surprisingly, many clients are quite unforgiving of these mistakes—and the bad results that follow from them. In addition, because we lawyers frequently represent clients suing people for *their* mistakes, when the lawyer makes a mistake, it's only natural and ironically appropriate that his client will sue him.

We also fear losing clients when we refuse to lie for them. Clients will often lie about the existence of documents and destroy or alter them. A physician has told me of instances when doctors on call to hospital emergency rooms have caused patient deaths by neglecting to answer their pages—and then have colluded with hospital personnel to alter or destroy the medical records documenting that negligence. Most lawyers who have been in litigation practice for any length of time can tell similar stories.

A recent client asked if a document that contained a certain phrase would help his case. I said, "Yes, it would." Several days later, the document conveniently appeared. My suspicions aroused, I determined conclusively that the document was a forgery. When confronted by it, the client brazenly swore that the document was authentic. I fired the client. Under the circumstances, I couldn't help burning a bridge.

---

[11] Although Thompson's words made an indelible mental impression on me, I have been unable to find the actual article in which they appeared.

In another matter, a client wanted to avoid having a lease cancelled and asked me what would happen if the lease renewal he'd neglected to send in on time were to be backdated. I told him that backdating a document was improper. I have not heard from him since.

Besides fearing that we'll lose clients, lawyers also fear being ostracized by our peers. The profession promotes a "gang" mentality—if we want to be an accepted member, we have to do as other members of the gang do. This mentality is part of what caused me not to demur when my colleague John destroyed evidence. If someone I respected did it, then it must be okay; and if I didn't go along, I wouldn't be permitted to continue being a member of the club. This phenomenon was observable in two workshops that I conducted in consecutive years with young lawyers. In each, I asked them to role-play a young associate confronting a particular moral dilemma. The first year, I stipulated that the associate experienced no pressure to be unethical from a senior partner. Even so, 33% were patently unethical because they feared admitting an embarrassing and potentially costly mistake. In the second year, when I did stipulate that additional pressure, over 90% were patently unethical.

I am not suggesting that the fears that incite lawyers to lie are unique to the legal profession. History shows us numerous examples in which individuals' fear of losing status in their group contributes to lying (e.g., the Nixon White House, the savings-and-loan industry of the mid- and late-'80s). Other occupational settings have their own sets of fears, some similar to, and some different from, those that cause lawyers to lie.

For now, I'm simply saying that lying in litigation arises out of fear. Whether it's fear of humiliation, losing, economic loss, ostracism by our peers, or whatever else, if we didn't fear some consequence of telling the truth, we'd have no need to lie.

Systemic Influences

Lying always occurs in a context, not in a vacuum. As hard as it may be to accept, no lawyer I know awakens, looks in the mirror, and says, "What clever, bald-faced lies can I tell today just for the sake of lying?" Rather, there are powerful systemic factors that encourage lawyers to lie. Let's look at a few.

The XY Game

The rules were deceptively simple. The players, of which I was one, were divided into several groups of 4. The object of the game: "Win as much as you can." The game was played in ten successive rounds. At the beginning of each, we had a choice of secretly circling either an X or a Y on a slip of paper. The basic payoff schedule was as follows:

4 X's — *lose $1.00 each*
3 X's, 1 Y — *X's win $1.00 each, Y loses $3*
2 X's, 2 Y's — *X's win $2 each, Y's lose $2 each*
1 X, 3 Y's — *X wins $3, Y's lose $1 each*
4 Y's — *win $1 each*

We'd also have bonus rounds in which the results were multiplied by 3 (round 5), 5 (round 8), and 10 (round 10).

Analyzing the payoff schedule, I quickly saw that if everyone in my group played Y, we'd all win. If everyone played X, we'd all lose. And if some played X and some played Y, the X's would win at the Ys' expense. I resolved to find a way to get everyone in my group to play Y.

For the first three rounds, no one was allowed to talk. In the first round, two of my foursome circled Y and two circled X. In the second and third rounds, three circled X and I circled Y, figuring I might lead the others by example into a win/win situation. I hoped to obtain their cooperation by showing that I had no desire to take advantage of them. Before the fourth round, our game leader gave each group permission to discuss their strategy. All members of my own group agreed to circle Y during the fourth round. But when the results were tabulated, we had three Y's and one X. The lone X came from Randy, who'd apparently figured that if everyone played Y, he'd win just a dollar, whereas if everyone else played Y and he played X, he'd win three dollars.

Incredulous at his greediness, I said, "If you keep doing that, I'm gonna f—— you." But in round 5, Randy shamelessly circled X again, as did another member. I, meanwhile, hoping that my

*threat plus my own willingness to "take the high road" would
cause Randy and the others to cooperate, played Y, as did the
remaining group member. In round six, everyone, including me,
righteously carrying out my threat, played X, and consequently
all of us lost a dollar. But, by God, Randy didn't win!*

*Before round seven, we were again allowed to discuss strat-
egy. This time, everyone, including Randy, who apparently
decided that the rest of us wouldn't let him continue to "victimize" us, agreed to play Y. In round seven, everyone did, in fact,
play Y.*

*Round eight brought us our second bonus round, with the
stakes at five times the amount of the original wager. This time,
Randy brazenly played "X" again while the rest of us played Y!
He won $15; we each lost $5. In round nine, Randy tried to
sucker us yet again. His strategy was to play a repentant Y in
order to lead us to believe that he would also play a Y in round
10, the last bonus round. This was a repeat of the strategy he'd
used in rounds seven and eight. This time, the rest of the group
didn't buy the hustle and all of us except Randy played X in
round nine. We each won a dollar while Randy lost $3.*

*In round 10, everyone, including Randy, played X, with the
result that all four of us lost $10.*

Cooperation vs. Competition

The XY Game, which has been played in corporate
training rooms for many years and which I played at a
weekend workshop on money issues, is a metaphor for the
win/lose nature of the legal system (and our system of
commerce, for that matter). Lawsuits begin because someone (now called the defendant) has done something that
someone else (now called the plaintiff) perceives to be at
his or her expense. The plaintiff then sues for financial
compensation—and sometimes for punitive damages as
well. On the face of it, such a situation does not look
promising for cooperation between the two parties, but in
fact, as Parts II and III explain, cooperation *is* possible. Or,
to put it another way, both parties *can* play Y. They just
aren't conscious of the choice.

First, though, I want to examine why "up-and-downsmanship"—engaging in one-up/one-down conflict where

the sole object is to prevail over one another—persists in the legal system, and, in turn, how it engenders lying.

Lawyers and non-lawyers alike play X, even when Y would be more consistent with our ultimate objectives. Of the more than 70 people who attended the money workshop that I've just described, only two of us were lawyers, yet almost all of the foursomes contained X players like Randy. Another workshop, this one for several hundred entering MBA students at the University of Texas, turned up similar results in a similar game. There, most of the players often chose X strategies even when Y strategies would have produced more consistently favorable results. It's pretty obvious, then, that the legal system is not alone in operating on a fiercely competitive basis. It reflects a cultural tendency toward one-up/one-down competition—but carried to its logical extreme. To fail to recognize that the civil-justice system exists within a broader context is to limit potential remedies for lying and other repugnant behavior.

One fear that keeps lawyers from cooperating with one another is that when the stakes are high—i.e., at trial—the opposing lawyer, who may have lulled us into a sense of false security, will suddenly play X, just as Randy did during the "bonus" rounds. I recall, for example, an auto-collision case that I once tried. The other lawyer, cordial and accommodating, cooperated with me throughout the pre-trial process. He was equally cordial during the trial itself. But, at one point, when he informed the judge that his client's mother had died, the judge specifically instructed him not to mention that fact to the jury. It was not relevant to the case, the judge said, and would make the jury unfairly sympathetic to his client. So what did the lawyer do? During his final argument, he brazenly informed the jury that his client's mother had died. And the judge's concern was borne out. Jurors later expressed more sympathy for the defendant than for my client, who was the injured victim!

The XY Game also illustrates our culture's tendency to default to competitive behavior and overlook the payoffs of cooperative strategies. Although some members of the two workshops went for the cooperative strategy without prompting, most played X's. Intuitively, most of the group members probably wanted to play Y to cooperate, but all it took was one person out of four to convert the "cooperators" into distrustful, aggressive competitors.

My experience with lawyers is similar. Most of us did not start out the way we have become. We started out with a human desire to like other people and have them like us, to find ways to get along and to cooperate. But something happened along the way. Sometimes it was another lawyer insisting on playing X's and being up-front about it; at other times, it was lawyers feinting Y and playing X. Regardless, the lesson was the same: we cannot trust one another.

Benjamin Sells, in *The Soul of the Law*, discusses what he calls "the litigious mind." An outgrowth of legal education and the law's adversary system, it shuts out cooperative strategies. Sells bemoans the litigator's reaction to mediation (a process by which a neutral person helps settle disputes):

> The steadfast and collective rejection of mediation by the litigators raises questions about the ability of an adversarial, litigation-based system to comprehend and appreciate the possibility of alternative approaches to resolving conflict. It seemed as if the litigators didn't want mediation to be a good idea, that it was being shot on the ground without being given a chance to fly. (Sells 85)

Thus, because of our conditioning—the emphasis on competitive strategies, both inside and outside of the legal system, and the disappointments we have experienced— we overlook cooperative strategies, even when they may be more effective in achieving our goals.

Remaining in a one-up/one-down system subjects us to at least two dynamics that encourage lying—and other repugnant behavior, for that matter. First, a win/lose system tends to objectify the opponent. When people are committed to working cooperatively, they must relate to each other and forge a bond of trust. In order to play Y, everyone had to trust that their colleagues would do likewise. In such a relationship, we look for the humanity in others and tend to treat them with humanity. In win/lose, however, the opponent becomes simply an object to prevail over. There's no need to relate or trust; you simply play the game. If the goal of the game is pure selfishness— to "win as much as you can"—the game places no value on treating opponents as fellow human beings. In retrospect, I don't think Randy felt that he was doing something wrong to any *person*; he was just playing the game. The rest of us were simply opponents to him—as remote as the faceless "subjects" of the Yale "learning" experiment discussed earlier. It's relatively easy to lie and engage in other repugnant behavior when your victim is not perceived in human terms.

Second, win/lose systems inexorably push participants to the edge of propriety. If the object is to beat an opponent, and if the rules of the game afford the only limits on how to do that, every incentive is to stretch the rules. The thinking is, if you don't do it, your opponent will. We see this tendency with "salary cap" shenanigans in professional football, attempts by overzealous alums to confer perks on college athletes, and the use of performance-enhancing drugs. When we tread on the edge of propriety, it's easy to overstep the line, as Randy and others did in the XY Game.

Interestingly, by the end of the workshop, among all the participants, Randy had become the *leading advocate* for using cooperative strategies. We'll look at factors that influenced his change of heart in Part II.

Just as the win/lose dynamics of the legal system embody a pervasive cultural attribute, so too does lying itself. Moreover, the examples in this chapter illustrate that, while the levels of justification vary, the legal process is replete with lying and deception, beginning with our clients.

This phenomenon is reflected in the following statement by Charles Curtis in *The Ethics of Advocacy* (Bok 146): "I don't see why we should not come out roundly and say that one of the functions of the lawyer is to lie for his client...." Moreover, one of my mentors has remarked more than once that "the difference between those of us who are ethical and those of us who are not is not whether we lie,

but what we lie about." I believe he meant that some lies—
like those in settlement negotiations, for example, which
"we all do"—are OK, but that others—lies that would
amount to fraud or perjury, for example—are not.[12]

Thus, one of the systemic influences on lying in the
legal system is that lying is a *norm*. It's an insidious development. We lawyers start by justifying it in circumstances
in which "everybody does it." Then, once on the slippery
slope of justification, we find it easy to rationalize lying in
more and more circumstances. Eventually, it becomes so
commonplace that we're now unconscious of it.

The process of justification is at the very heart of the
adversary system. Our clients rarely come to us and ask us
to help them take responsibility for wrongs they have
done to others. Such a prospect, unfortunately, is almost
laughable. Instead, they challenge us to find a way to
make them "right." We do this with great cleverness by
finding, or inventing, justification for their conduct. This
ingrained process of justification comes in handy when
we need an excuse to lie.

Another systemic influence on lying is that the adversarial process detaches the lawyer from the truth. Our
code of ethics prevents us from even stating our belief in
our client's cause. We are only permitted to argue that the
evidence presented justifies a conclusion; we are not permitted to express our own belief (or lack of belief) in our
position. For example, we can say that the client's
demeanor and the consistency of his or her story with
other facts makes the client worthy of belief. We cannot
say "*I believe* Bubba when he says...." In addition, what
really happened is history when the client comes to the
lawyer. The lawyer for each side presents a *version* of what
happened—in legal jargon, their own "theory" of the
case—and the judge or jury is left the task of divining the
truth from the competing versions.

[12] Ironically, some lawyers appear to think fraud in settlement negotiations
is justifiable. In a recent class action settlement agreement, the defense
lawyers inserted a provision that would prevent a plaintiff from suing for
fraud committed by the defense lawyers in procuring the settlement.

The system also ingrains in lawyers that the truth is anything for which we can make a case. I remember as a young lawyer fretting about whether I would be able to win a particular trial. After mentally reviewing all the arguments on both sides, I decided to bounce some ideas off my law clerk. I told her that I had argued with myself till I was blue in the face and still couldn't figure out whether I would win. She innocently asked, "Well, will you win if the jury believes what you think really happened?" Her question momentarily threw me off balance. I realized that the arguments I had been making had been attempts to reconstruct reality—from the perspective of my client and from that of the defendant. I had not looked at the facts objectively; I had not been thinking about what *really* happened. Upon realizing my folly, I answered, "Yes," and was reassured. But I was taken aback because I had been thinking about only what I could make a case for rather than what had *really* happened.

Another thing in our legal system that encourages lying is the constant blaming of others. Not only do we make a career of justifying our clients' often questionable conduct, but we also make a career of finding reasons to blame the other side. The underlying message in almost every trial is that something was the other side's *fault*. Over time, then, we lawyers become experts at listening for the lies of others and turning stone-deaf to our own.

The Personal Cost

I have hardly been immune to the justifications, the fear, and the systemic influences just discussed. For years, I was quick to see the lies of others and blind to my own. I also found it hard to see truth apart from whatever I could make a case for. Fear and facile justifications had the predictable effect: lying became a norm for me. Once I became conscious of what I was doing, as I'll be explaining in Chapter 10, I realized that almost every time I turned around, a lie would slip out of my mouth; it always seemed far easier to lie than to tell the truth.

I remember one trial years ago in which the opposing lawyer and I had a sidebar discussion with the judge, a sweet and kindly old gentleman, about whether certain evidence would be admitted before the jury. The judge decided that, no, the evidence was not to be admitted. Turning then to the jury, I proceeded to concoct some lie to tell them, my hope being to save face in light of the court's ruling. When I sprang the lie, I could see genuine sadness and disappointment in the judge's eyes. Later, and out of the hearing of the jury, he firmly and without judgment confronted me with my lie, and, with lawyerly sincerity,[13] I duly apologized.

At the time, I intuitively knew that there would not be "unacceptable" consequences. I think I saw the judge as a somewhat doddering old man whom I could manipulate. In retrospect, I am haunted by the specter of those kindly old eyes representing the fatherly disappointment in a generation gone astray and reflecting what became my own grave disappointment in myself.

Being a lawyer was easy as long as I didn't concern myself with what was right and wrong. More accurately, it was easy as long as I didn't examine my *own* behavior in light of my *own* professed standards of what is right and wrong. However, once I became conscious of my lack of integrity, living with it became untenable.

The Societal Cost

Aside from the injustice that results when litigants get away with lies, and aside from the costs of righting the wrongs in cases in which lies are discovered, lies carry another enormous cost: they perpetuate social disconnection. With few exceptions, when we lie or "merely" deceive, we treat one another as objects. And when we do that, we're opening wide the door to unproductive conflict, as we shall see.

---

[13] Although lawyers will understand this term, its meaning may not be clear to lay people. Lawyerly sincerity is behaving *as if* we are sincere.

CHAPTER 2

GETTING PHYSICAL

Trial lawyers are testy—often literally. A Georgia State University professor has determined that male trial lawyers, on average, have a higher level of testosterone than other lawyers.

Sometimes this testiness boils over, as it did when attorney Beavis Pelo, a highly competent but contentious plaintiff's lawyer, was taking a sworn statement of an expert witness for the defendant, Taylor Chemical Company, in front of a court reporter. Pelo's objective was to learn what the expert, Mr. Merdrock, would say at the trial so that Mr. Pelo could prepare his attack. Mr. Butch Cabezon was another lawyer on the plaintiff's side. The defense lawyers were Mr. Bo Dreckum and Ms. Sally Mentsch.

QUESTIONS BY MR. PELO:

Q. *(By Mr. Pelo) Tell me your full name, please, sir.*
A. *Jim Willie Merdrock.*

* * *

Q. *You were employed at one time by the Taylor Chemical Company?*
A. *Yes.*

* * *

Q. *And for what other companies have you done work for since Taylor?*
A. *These are—these are consulting contracts with me between me and these companies.*

Q. *Which companies are they?*

A. *I'm not sure that's germane.*

Q. *I'll decide that. What companies are they?*

A. *I think the companies should have the right to object.*

Q. *Are you refusing to answer the question?*

A. *I don't know. I don't know where I stand. Maybe I should get my lawyer and bring him over here.*

Q. *Are you taking the Fifth Amendment to that question?*

A. *No. I just think that maybe those people have the right to some privacy, don't you think?*

Q. *Is it some secret thing you're doing?*

A. *Absolutely not.*

Q. *Is it illegal?*

A. *No.*

Q. *Then who are they?*

A. *Well, you want to make an issue of it, okay. I'll make an issue of it, but I'm not going to tell you who my clients are.*

Q. *There are other defendants in this case other than Taylor.*

A. *It has absolutely nothing to do with any of them, with Texas, or anything else.*

Q. *You can't make that decision. You cannot make that decision.*

A. *All right, whatever you want to do about it. I will not tell you the name of my other clients.*

Q. *Are they oil companies?*

A. *Yes.*

Q. *Chemical companies?*

A. *No.*

*   *   *

Q. *What kind of companies do you represent?*

A. *Oh, various types.*

Q. *Tell me about them. What kind?*

A. *I don't think that's proper.*

Q. *Sir, you're not the judge of that. It wasn't proper for you to allow them to dump that toxic sludge in that dump.*

A. *Why don't you stop your incipient —*

MR. DRECKUM: *Hold it. I'm going to object to the sidebar, and I'm going to object to the responsiveness of the witness' answer as well. If you want some facts, just ask him what he knows.*

MR. PELO: *I'm asking.*

Q. *(By Mr. Pelo) Who are the companies?*

A. *I'll consult with my attorneys when we have a break.*

Q. *Consult with him now.*

A. *No. I have a private attorney. It happens to be my son who works for a firm here in the county.*

Q. *Go out there and call him. Go out there and call him.*

MR. DRECKUM: *Let's go off the record.*

MR. PELO: *No, we don't go off the record.*

MR. DRECKUM: *Let's go off the record.*

Q. *(By Mr. Pelo) You go call him?*

A. *Right now let's don't do that. Let's get this thing over with.*

Q. *You're not going to go call him?*

A. *No.*

MR. DRECKUM: *Hold on just a second. Wait a minute.*

A. *I'll call him afterwards.*

Q. *(By Mr. Pelo) That's too late.*

MR. DRECKUM: *Let's make the record real clear. Mr. Pelo, I thought you said let's go off the record and have him call him.[14] Now, if you're going to have him ask that question and give him an opportunity to do that, that's fine.*

MR. PELO: *He won't go.*

MR. DRECKUM: *Well, you invited him to go off the record and make the phone call.*

Q. *(By Mr. Pelo) Did you talk to this man [Dreckum] sitting next to you before this deposition got started?*

A. *Yesterday, but he had nothing to do with this.*

Q. *I didn't ask you that.*

A. *I said it, though, didn't I?*

Q. *Did you talk to him, sir? What did you say?*

A. *I said nothing. I said you have a case of incipient verbal diarrhea.*

Q. *Oh, sir, we're going to see about that.*

A. *Well, good.*

* * *

---

[14] Although Mr. Pelo never actually suggested going off the record, he did so implicitly when he suggested that the witness go out and call his son. Doing so would have required temporarily stopping the deposition.

Q. ... Now, Mr. Merdrock, tell me the nature of the business,
    the companies with whom you consult, what's the nature of
    their business?

A. They sell products on the market.

Q. What kind of products?

A. All kinds of products.

Q. Name some of them.

A. I don't think I should identify them for you, and I will not.
    Now, if there's anything legal about that or I have to go to
    jail, I'll do that.[15]

Q. Why do you feel like you have something to hide?

MR. DRECKUM: Object to the form of the question.

A. Because I am giving a deposition to you in connection with
    a case in Texas concerning the Junction City plant. I cannot
    see for any reason why that has anything to do with or ger-
    mane to what particular customers or clients I've consulted
    for.

Q. (By Mr. Pelo) If we get into what you can't see, we may be
    here a long time.

MR. DRECKUM: Object to the side bar. If you've got questions,
    ask him.

* * *

Q. And was that your title during your entire stay at Junction
    City?

A. At Junction City, yes.

MR. DRECKUM: Don't talk over each other.

Q. (By Mr. Pelo) After you left Junction City—

MR. CABEZON: Wait a minute. Let me ask a question here.
    Do you represent this guy or not?

MR. DRECKUM: Who are you?

MR. CABEZON: My name's Cabezon, and I represent Ducator,
    and I just want to know do you represent the guy or not?
    I'm getting, you know, if you don't represent him, you don't
    have any right to be making any objections. If you do repre-
    sent him, tell us so.

MR. DRECKUM: Why don't you keep your mouth shut, and I'll
    do what I want.

---

[15] Merdrock is probably not within his rights here: who his other clients are,
possibly *all* defendants and no plaintiffs, would be relevant to showing his bias.

MR. CABEZON: *No, you're not going to do what you want.*
MR. PELO: *No way.*
MR. DRECKUM: *Yeah, I am.*
MR. PELO: *That's bullshit.*
MR. DRECKUM: *I'll make whatever objections I want to make, and I'll make them as loud as I want to make them. Now, you just shut your mouth and we'll keep the record straight.*
MR. CABEZON: *Don't tell me to shut my mouth, Boy. You may be big, but you want to see how bad you are, come on.*
MR. PELO: *And I wouldn't try that, Bo.*
THE WITNESS: *Are you threatening to fight?*
MR. DRECKUM: *Hold on just a second.*
THE WITNESS: *No, I want to know whose side I'm on. We're going to be out-numbered, Bo.*
MR. DRECKUM: *Hold on just a second.*
MR. PELO: *No. You got a big mouth. Now, you do. You either need to represent the man or not.*
MR. DRECKUM: *I'm representing Taylor Chemical, and I'm making an objection on the record.*
MR. PELO: *Then you're not entitled to be his lawyer then, okay?*
MR. DRECKUM: *I'm not representing the man. I'm making an objection on the record.*
MR. PELO: *And another thing, I'm going to tell you something else. You don't run this deposition, you understand?*
MR. DRECKUM: *Neither do you, Beavis.*
MR. PELO: *You watch and see. You watch and see who does, Big Boy.*
MR. DRECKUM: *I'm telling you, Beavis, I'm going to make whatever objections I want to make. You can talk as loud as you want—*
MR. PELO: *And don't be telling other lawyers to shut up. That isn't your goddamned job, Fat Boy.*
MR. DRECKUM: *Well, that's not your job, Mr. Hairpiece.*
THE WITNESS: *As I said before, you have an incipient—*
MR. PELO: *What do you want to do about it, asshole?*
THE WITNESS: *I'd like to knock you on your ass.*
MR. PELO: *Come over here and try it, you dumb son of a bitch. Come over here.*

MR. DRECKUM: *Hold it. No way.*
THE WITNESS: *You couldn't even get close.*
MR. DRECKUM: *Hold on just a second. You're not going to bully this guy.*
MR. PELO: *Oh, you big fat tub of shit, sit down.*
MR. DRECKUM: *I don't care how many of you come up against me—*
MR. PELO: *Oh, you big fat tub of shit, sit down. Sit down, you fat tub of shit.*
THE WITNESS: *Why don't you shut up once in a while and be honest and decent. If you want me to, I will answer your questions.*
MS. MENTSCH: *All right. Let's go off the record for about five minutes and everybody calm down.*
(Whereupon, a conversation was held off the record.)

Provocation/Response in Kind

What you have just read is part of an actual deposition taken in a large Texas city. Texas, testosterone, and trial lawyers are a prescription for incivility. What's surprising about the transcribed events is not that they occurred, but that similar events do not occur more often.[16] The context for this particular deposition was a lawsuit in which it was alleged that catastrophic injuries had been visited upon the plaintiffs by a chemical company. In early times, if a neighbor had poisoned a member of one's family, "an eye for an eye" was the operative principle and self-help was the method. Now the most violent emotions arising from wrongs, both grievous and small, are channelled into a legal system that seeks to contain them like sandbags retaining raging floodwaters. When Americans get angry enough to kill and don't want to suffer the consequences, they do the next best thing: they hire a lawyer. The opposition perceives the threat and responds with equivalent

---

[16] Among the panoply of factors that rein in such grossly excessive hostility are the fear of monetary sanctions, a modicum of impulse control, the professional socialization process that discourages such behavior, and recognition that such hostility may hurt our own clients and our own chances for success.

fury. Called upon to act out the emotions of our clients, we lawyers are the instruments of savage instincts.

In 1990, while doing a nationwide computer search for articles about lawyers engaging in actual fistfights, *The Texas Lawyer* weekly turned up over 100 articles published in the early-to-mid '90s that carried the word "fight" in them, indicative of the way we equate litigation with physical fighting.

In addition, there were a few examples, as one might imagine, of actual physical fights. In a lawsuit filed over a 1993 incident, one Maryland attorney alleged that an opposing lawyer "grabbed [him] by the shirt collar and necktie with his hands in an attempt to strangle [him]...." The complaint further alleged that the defendant lawyer threw the plaintiff lawyer into a wall, creating a hole eight inches wide. The defendant lawyer claimed that he "didn't lose [his] temper" but only came to the defense of a female associate whom he thought was being assaulted.

In San Francisco, there was an instance of two lawyers getting into a fistfight and of another lawyer being shot through the neck by a defendant in a civil case.

The Texas Lawyer carried this report on June 17, 1996:

> Corporate defense attorneys say a deposition in Rockwall County got way out of hand when Dallas plaintiffs' attorney L.L. "Mick" McBee physically attacked a Chrysler attorney on May 8. In an affidavit filed in 382d District Court in Rockwall, Roy A. Spezia, a shareholder in Austin's Clark, Thomas & Winters, claims he was the victim of an "unprovoked attack" when McBee "grabbed me with both hands around my shoulders and threw me into a wooden cabinet that was up against a wall." . . . "I've seen quite a few civil suits up here, but I've never seen two sides hate each other more," says Rick Calvert, a Rockwall County assistant D.A. ("Uncivil Suit" 3)

With such intense emotions driving lawsuits, lawyers will often get caught up in them and act them out. Sometimes they're asked to, very directly, as when a client asks the lawyer to make the opposition miserable. "There is this push to kill your adversary at all costs," says Laureen De Buono, an in-house counsel for a California manufacturing firm. "It's definitely part of the litigation beast, and you have to find ways to deal with it" ("Separating the Just" 27). "It's a matter of principle!" the livid client will protest. "I just want justice!" The lawyer gets the point: It's war.

Recently, some particularly angry clients hired me to help them take over a homeowners' association that controlled the roads and amenities in their subdivision. I suggested a number of cooperative strategies that I believed would achieve the substantive results they wanted. At each mention of such a strategy, though, they expressed angry defensiveness, as if I were on the other side. I soon found myself making uncharacteristically warlike statements to reassure them that I really was on their side. Once I'd shown my willingness to *fight* for them, they seemed reassured. Their angry energy needed an outlet; if I was unwilling to be that outlet, I was not going to be their lawyer.

The indirect pressure to "act out" is in the nature of the adversary system itself. The two fundamental elements of the system are a *provocation* and a *response in kind*. Plaintiffs sue because they have been provoked by a perceived wrong. Defendants see the mere act of the other side's hiring a lawyer as provocative in itself, and so begins the pattern of provocation and response in kind. As we lawyers orchestrate this dance for our clients, we become participants in the dance itself and begin to take personally the actions of opposing counsel. Pretty soon, everyone touched by the adversary system is involved, including witnesses.

Let me give you another example of this provocation/response dynamic. This one occurred during a deposition in a suit over a defective heart valve. Mr. Eastwood, the plaintiff's lawyer, asked questions for five pages before the defense witness acknowledged that, yes, the heart valve had malfunctioned, a fact about which there was no genuine dispute. The defense lawyer continued to obstruct Eastwood during the entire deposition until the following exchange occurred:

EASTWOOD: Don't ever accuse me of misrepresenting.
HALEY: I'll accuse you of whatever I want to.
EASTWOOD: No, you won't, Dirk, or I'll knock the shit out of you.

A third example of "getting physical" occurred during a trial in central Texas. Jack Roffelo, an Austin attorney who gained fame as a criminal defense lawyer, squared off against P.T. Switcher, a highly paid corporate lawyer and former public office-holder. Switcher, according to Roffelo, had repeatedly used "speaking objections." In other words, instead of simply objecting to evidence based on a specific ground such as relevance or hearsay, Switcher would interject speeches that, in Roffelo's view, were insufferably long-winded. After one such speaking objection, Roffelo leaned over to Switcher and in a loud whisper said, "P.T., if you do that one more time, I'm gonna kick your ass." Overhearing the remark, a juror, in his own stage whisper, said, "Hit him, Jack!"

In all these instances, there was a perceived provocation. Pelo, for example, was not only provoked by the witness's remark about "incipient case of verbal diarrhea" but by what he perceived as the witness's stonewalling. He complained shortly after the intermission that "We started this deposition unable to get an answer from this man."

As for Eastwood's troubles with Haley, the provocation was stonewalling, a term that bears further definition. In many complex cases involving defective products, medical malpractice, anti-trust, and the like, plaintiffs must prove significant elements of their case through the records or witnesses of the defendant. Many defense lawyers, encouraged by their clients, make it as difficult as possible for the plaintiffs to find the "smoking guns." Some do this by means of "stonewalling"—by interrupting, stalling, objecting, quibbling, and instructing witnesses in the art of convenient amnesia. Plaintiff's lawyers can quickly grow exasperated dealing with such tactics; it feels like banging one's head against granite.

In the case involving Roffelo and Switcher, the immediate provocation was windy objections exacerbated by the heat of trial. Lawyers in trial often survive on little sleep for weeks on end. I recall one three-and-a-half-week case I tried against two lawyers who happened to office in my own building. Night after night, I'd finally drag out about midnight, only to find that their lights were still on. My heart would sink. I just knew they would be concocting fresh ways to stick it to me the next day. But I'd get to crow when I'd observe their lights out upon my return at 4:30 a.m. When emotions are raw and lawyers are sleep-deprived, it doesn't take much to provoke.

This is especially true in long trials. In a very complex state court case, one lawyer approached another to begin a fight right in front of the judge. The daily transcript read as follows:

> THE COURT...wait a minute we are big boys no wait just a minute. We are all big boys and we are all professionals. This is not going to happen in this Court. Not in the presence of the jury and the Court now back off and stand over here....

The Enemy Within

These instances of getting physical illustrate something common to all areas of lying and other repugnant behavior, both for lawyers and non-lawyers alike: part of us not only approves of but *admires* much of what we self-righteously criticize. I have to confess, for example, that when I heard about Roffelo telling Switcher that he'd kick his ass, I not only thought it was a cool thing to do, I wished I had the machismo to kick ass myself. I love Clint Eastwood westerns just like most of the population. None of this stopped me, though, from nodding in self-righteous agreement when some of my fellow writers of the Texas Lawyers Creed disparaged lawyers who would stoop to threats of physical violence. These scribes probably felt some hypocrisy themselves. Wanting so much to project an image of professionalism, we all resisted 'fessing up to the parts of ourselves that undercut that image. We were judging others guilty of what we found most difficult to accept in ourselves. Another word for this is *scapegoating*, the same phenomenon that generates lawyer-bashing.

When Republicans bash Democrats for profligate spending, they forget the huge deficits run up by the Reagan administration. When Democrats bash Republicans for wasteful military buildups, they forget the cost of their favorite pork-barrel military bases. When one spouse bashes the other for not paying attention to his or her needs, he or she forgets that this very bashing ignores the other spouse's needs. When we lawyers bash each other for lying and other repugnant behavior, we forget our own lying and other repugnant behavior. Bashing is a form of scapegoating.

Bashing is also just another form of justifying and blaming. The lawyer response to bashing is usually to justify and blame in return. For example, a recent television program called *The Trouble with Lawyers* spent almost an hour faulting lawyers. The typical lawyer response, including the one from the president of the State Bar Board on which I served, wasn't concessionary. It was merely a complaint that the program did not emphasize all of the good things that lawyers do.

Unless we lawyers begin to acknowledge responsibility for our part in what's wrong with the civil-justice system, we can expect to continue to be bashed. As Chapter 6 illustrates, the only way to guarantee a satisfactory result to a conflict, be it a lawsuit or broadside attacks on lawyers as a group, is to begin by owning our own responsibility for the problem.

CHAPTER 3

HARDBALL

Lawyers...they're like nuclear warheads.
They have theirs, so I have mine. Once you use
'em, they f— up everything.
—From the movie *Other People's Money*

Although lawyers can "get physical" with one another, both verbally (through threats) and bodily, it's not too common. What *is* common, though, is "hardball." Hardball consists of non-physical, hostile tactics aimed simply at punishing the other side, irrespective of the client's ultimate objectives.[17]

In the trade, we call them "Rambo tactics."

The Texas Lawyers Creed[18] gives a pretty complete picture of the various forms that hardball can take. Among other things, the Creed exhorts lawyers to:

- Avoid quarreling over matters of form.
- Prepare documents that actually reflect the agreement that the parties reached.
- Avoid serving motions at the last minute in order to prevent the other side from adequately preparing.
- Avoid antagonistic or obnoxious behavior.
- Avoid disparaging remarks or acrimony towards opposing counsel, parties, and witnesses.
- Avoid alluding to "personal peculiarities or idiosyncrasies of opposing counsel."
- Avoid being influenced by any ill feeling between clients.

---

[17] Lawyers consider most of our face-to-face encounters to be civil. The instances in which friction occurs, however, have an impact greater than their frequency would suggest. Clients, moreover, take offense to much that lawyers consider "civil."

[18] I have attached a copy as Appendix A.

- Avoid arbitrarily scheduling depositions and court appearances without consulting the opposing counsel.
- Stipulate to undisputed facts so that the other side will not have to incur unnecessary costs.
- Refrain from excessive and abusive discovery.
- Avoid making objections or giving instructions to a witness for the purpose of delaying or obstructing.
- Avoid encouraging a witness to fail to understand a question or to quibble about words.
- Avoid resisting (stonewalling) discovery requests that are reasonable.
- Avoid seeking sanctions unless necessary to protect a client's lawful objectives.

Here, then, is hardball: stonewalling, quibbling, delaying, obstructing, abusive discovery, disparaging remarks, acrimony, and antagonistic or obnoxious behavior.

Win at All Costs

This behavior stems from the very structure of the adversary system. Lawyers are trained to assume that any tactic permitted by the law is not only moral but morally *required*. Those of us who graduated law school before the early '80s—and in some areas of the country even until 1990—were taught that we are professionally obliged to represent our clients "zealously within the bounds of the law."[19] Because the word "zealously" was found to promote overly aggressive tactics, it has been dropped from the canons of legal ethics. Nonetheless, the attitude persists among lawyers that we are duty-bound to be aggressive.

In every lawsuit, we begin with what I call a "game assumption"—that is, the collection of unspoken rules of engagement governing the particular game (contest of wits) we are playing with the other lawyer. The game assumption will normally crystallize in response to a

---

[19] The 1975 version of Canon 7 of the ABA Model Code of Ethics was revised to omit the "zealous" requirement in 1983. See, also, TEX. CODE PROF. RESP., Art. 10, sec. 9, can. 7, *reprinted in* TEX. GOV'T CODE ANN., tit. 2, subtit. G. app. (Vernon 1984), superseded 1990.

"provocation" and will often bring us to mutter, with eyes flashing, "Oh, so *that's* the game we're gonna play!" At such times, the game assumption amounts to this:

> *We shall use every means permitted by the*
> *rules of procedure to clobber the opposition.*

Such an assumption—sometimes called the "win/ lose" game assumption—is entirely competitive. Note that it omits any mention of the client's objectives. Note, too, that it rules out compromise. It requires using *every* means permitted by the rules, however inefficient it may be.

Lawyers are not taught to ask, "What strategy will most effectively meet the client's objectives?" Why? Because our teaching emphasizes "winning." If carried out literally, the competitive game assumption would result in every case being tried. To "win," you'd have to prevail over the other side, and that would mean going to trial.

Escalation

Hostile actions toward opposing lawyers virtually never produce submission. Many of us are lawyers precisely because we never want to appear weak.

Such actions thus lead, instead, to escalation. Since most lawyers start out playing the "win/lose" game assumption, any show of hostility reinforces that assumption and triggers the provocation/response dynamic. Second, the message within each response is, "I'll show you not to mess with me by hitting you *harder* than you hit me." As a young lawyer, I was told to give other lawyers the benefit of the doubt, but if they "crossed the line"— that is, did something unfair—my superiors advised me to bar no holds.

Lawyers often remind me of those mortal enemies, the cat and the mouse, in a famous cartoon. First, they stand off and put up their fists. Then the mouse draws a knife. Then the cat grabs a pistol. Then the mouse whips out a rifle. Then the cat shoulders a bazooka. Moments later, the mouse materializes in a tank, whereupon the cat produces a battleship, to which the mouse responds with an H-bomb. What an eminently human progression!

Escalation, with lawyers, occurs in the "weapons" they use. If the other side has it, we must not only match it, we must trump it, be it with jury consultants, high-dollar professional expert witnesses on everything, computer graphics, video displays, multi-media presentations, computer-assisted research, computerized evidence databases, indices, and on and on. You saw it all in the O.J. Simpson criminal trial. The problem is that clients must pay for each fresh round of "hardware" to avoid being outgunned. Often, the costs of warfare outrun the potential spoils.

Escalation occurs not only in weaponry but in tactics and emotion. Each new provocation calls for a more extreme response. Judges recognize these disputes when they feel the urge to tell the lawyers to "go to your rooms." Lawyers know that they are in the midst of such an escalatory spiral when all they can think of at bedtime is, "How can I get back at that S.O.B.?"

Once again, clients are the ones who have to pay the tab for this silliness. I know of several divorce lawyers whose hiring will almost guarantee a protracted, costly battle because of the tendency to act out their clients' desires to escalate. If lawsuits begin with both lawyers cooperating, the cost will be far less than if the emotional escalation leads to hostile tactics.

Blaming and Justifying Revisited

Blaming and justifying accompany incivility as much as lying. The justification consists of a perceived provocation. We then blame others for bringing *our* hostility upon themselves! For example, the bar-room bully who uses an inconsequential slight to pick a fight might preface a left hook with, "Wuz you lookin' at mah wife?" The message: *You provoked me—so you're gonna get what you deserve!*

Justifications for hostility in the legal system may be more sophisticated, but no more valid. My own justifications for playing hardball came as easily as those for lying—and I started doing both, playing hardball and justifying it, right out of law school in my first job as an Assistant Attorney General. My assignment was to sue trade schools for violations of state laws. It was a practice at that time for many trade schools to take tuition from poor, unqualified students who lacked the prerequisites for academic success. Soon after enrolling, the students would inevitably flunk out. But the schools would often fail to refund the tuition, thereby flouting state law.

> *Enrique was a first-generation Texan whose parents had emigrated from Mexico. After dropping out of high school because of an inability to read English, Enrique enrolled in court-reporting school. His full two-year tuition was paid with his family's life savings because his parents wanted him to have a better life than they had. After three months, it became obvious to Enrique that high fluency in English was an undisclosed prerequisite to success in court-reporting school. Feeling abject failure, Enrique quit school and returned to manual labor, his family's mode of survival. The school retained the total tuition.*

I never knew an Enrique, but I enforced the Texas trade school laws with all the zeal of his champion. To me, the other side was evil and their lawyers simply co-conspirators. So I'd set hearings with no regard for the other side's convenience. Occasionally, I'd go even further, setting depositions on short notice or at times likely to be inconvenient to the other side. We were right, they were wrong, and we were gonna stick 'em. Compromise? Not with scoundrels like these! The ends justified the means.

In another case, where I was trying to collect a judgment against a shoddy builder, I justified my aggressive tactics because *we were right.* First, I sued his elderly wife to bring additional pressure. Then, I scheduled a court hearing for Monday at 8:00 a.m. without consulting the other side. My hope was that the opposing lawyer would forget to show up for the hearing and I'd win by default.

Hardball conduct can be either calculated or reflexive.

When it's calculated, it's designed to achieve a specific purpose. Although justified by a perceived provocation, it is future-oriented; it attempts to achieve a premeditated result. When I engaged in it, I rationalized it as necessary to further my clients' righteous objectives. I know a number of lawyers who still believe in trying to rattle or intimidate their opposition.

When hardball conduct is reflexive, on the other hand, it's lashing out in direct response to a perceived provocation. Hence, it is past-oriented. The distinction between calculated and reflexive conduct is akin to the distinction between premeditated murder and a crime of passion. Moreover, as with crimes of passion, some perpetrators are repentant and some are unrepentant. So, too, with lawyers who are reflexively uncivil.

In many cases, the incivility appears calculated when it is actually reflexive. Although some who know Mr. Pelo would argue that he has been guilty of calculated incivility, I believe it's the only way he knows how to be. Mr. Pelo's unconsciousness of his own incivility was evident in this statement that occurred immediately after the opposing parties left the room:

MR. PELO: *I want to say something on the record. Now Mr. Dreckum and his associate are taking Mr. Merdrock out in the hall to lecture him, I suppose. They're doing this over our objection. We started this deposition unable to get an answer from this man. It's been interrupted by the bombastic, unethical, unprofessional remarks of Mr. Dreckum to Mr. Cabezon and to me, and they've taken him away. We'll wait here until they bring him back, I suppose, if it's any reasonable time.*

It is difficult to see how Mr. Pelo could rationally claim that the other side's conduct was "unprofessional" without implicating his own. Only if he literally failed to hear himself do these statements make sense.

Consider, moreover, whether the incivility Mr. Pelo exhibits in the following excerpt from an unrelated case appears to be calculated or simply reflexive and unrepentant:

HEMPHILL: *Would you please repeat the question? I think between all of that dribble we lost it.*
PELO: *Read it to him, shit.*
TELLER: *Did you get that on the record?*

PELO: *We're going to put everything on, my love. We're going to stick it up your nose before it's over.*

Q: *(By Mr. Pelo) Did you answer the question?*

A: *No, sir.*

HASTINGS: *What was the question?*

PELO: *I forgot it. Read it back to him.*

HEMPHILL: *Well, Randy can tell it to you again.*

PELO: *Tell it to me again, Randy.*

A: *I will not answer on the basis of the invocation of the attorney-client privilege.*

PELO: *We want to certify that, too, please.*

Q: *(By Mr. Pelo) At the time this letter was written, April 4th, 1986, Tattler, Tinkford was also attorney of record for Hobart, Jr. and Kenny Baum, were they not?*

A: *Yes, sir.*

(Discussion off the Record)

PELO: *I want to certify the last question and answer.*

Q: *Let's talk about Donny Gerber for a while, give this lady [Ms. Teller] a thrill. There was substantial interest at the time, I take it, on the part of all the lawyers in the case and the parties of making sure that any person who had an interest in the case, in the Stassney family trust, were brought into the case. Is that your recollection or not, sir?*

HEMPHILL: *Excuse me. That would call for Mr. Harley to disclose privileged information.*

PELO: *Horseshit.*

Q: *(By Mr. Pelo) Go on and answer the question.*

A: *I'm not going to answer the question on the basis of the attorney-client privilege.*

Q: *Well, do you realize that the canons of ethics when you represent multiple parties of adverse interests frown on this sort of thing?*

TELLER: *Well, I object to that as not exactly a correct statement of what the canons of ethics —*

PELO: *Then you need to have some more semesters in ethics, my love.*

Q: *(By Mr. Pelo) Answer the question.*

HEMPHILL: *Frown on what sort of thing, Mr. Pelo? The question is unclear. Would you please try and be a little more specific?*

PELO: *It's clear.*

Q: *(By Mr. Pelo) Go ahead, Mr. Burney. And you keep looking*
     at him. He's not your lawyer. Is he going to signal you in
     some way? He can't infuse you with knowledge or bravery
     or anything? So, look at me and answer the question.
HASTINGS: *Do you understand the question?*
TELLER: *Mr. Pelo, I object.*
PELO: *When I get interested in what you think, I'll make you a*
     partner. Until then, you can kiss my ass, okay? Now, let's
     go ahead.
TELLER: *Boy, that's one thing I sure wouldn't want to do, sir.*
PELO: *It would be the best loving you ever had.*
TELLER: *I doubt it — I doubt it, Mr. Pelo.*
Q: *(By Mr. Pelo) Go ahead and answer the question.*
HEMPHILL: *Now let's get back —*
TELLER: *Pardon me, pardon me. I object.*
PELO: *I have pardoned you a long time ago.*
TELLER: *I object to your behavior in an abusive manner —*
PELO: *Oh, I feel like I'm in the principal's office now.*

The distinction between calculated and reflexive behavior is important for two reasons. That we lawyers assume uncivil behavior to be calculated when it is more often reflexive points up our tendency to blame rather than to assume any responsibility for fostering the conflict. If we acknowledge that someone is reflexively uncivil, we may be forced to look at the nature of our own conduct that triggered the "reflex."

Second, to assume that the conduct is calculated satisfies our desire for simplicity. If someone calculates to be uncivil, the simple solution is to "punish" the individual in some way, and to extinguish the behavior by promulgating a rule or by otherwise imposing unacceptable consequences. But if we consider the conduct reflexive, more complex approaches are suggested. We'll be asking sensible questions like: What triggered the reflex? If we are in fact the "provocateur," how might we modify our own behavior so as not to provoke further incivility? How do we go about achieving such change? Why is incivility the response to the trigger rather than a more adaptive response? How can we learn to respond more appropriately?

Fear in Disguise

Ironically, the hostility that looks so fearsome is merely fear in disguise. Whether calculated or reflexive, our incivility is prompted by our desire to feel strong and powerful. I have heard Mr. Pelo discuss the importance of "being the most powerful person" in the room. Lawyers hate showing weakness or appearing weak. The fact that we need to feel powerful at another's expense underscores our fears of weakness.

This fear of weakness is underlaid by an even deeper fear—of annihilation. Our experience tells us that if we show weakness, we risk being destroyed. My dream of being overrun when my weapon stopped working (Chapter 1) is a graphic example. Also, psychologist friends of mine tell me that a classic "lawyer-genic" family is one in which the imperious father debated with and humiliated his children at the dinner table. They learned that a weakness in their argument was immediately followed by a feeling of annihilation and humiliation. In the law, they seek a means to overpower others, so that they are never in a weak or one-down position. In law school this same dynamic may be replicated by law professors who call on and embarrass their students in class. After one of these experiences, law students can be heard to remark that they "almost died" in class—and they feel as if they did. How can they not associate weakness with annihilation?

When, as a beginning lawyer, I was representing the state with religious zeal, I was terrified (albeit unconsciously) of annihilation. If others perceived me as weak, I was sure I'd be victimized for my inexperience.

In one of the few divorce cases I've handled, my client, the husband, had discovered that his wife was having an affair. He wanted her thrown out of the house. I succeeded in getting a court order to do just that. Her lawyer, who has since gained a reputation as the most aggressive divorce lawyer in the county, counterattacked with such fury that I wanted to run and hide. That was the last divorce case I handled for 20 years.

The Professional Response

One problem with responding in kind, even when the other side is provocative, is that both sides look bad. As Jack Ratliff, a University of Texas Law School professor, likes to joke, "Never wrestle with a pig—you'll both get dirty, but the pig likes it." A better strategy is to take the dispute to the court, where the only issue is whether the other side's conduct was wrong—not whether one's own conduct or that of the opposition was worse.

Here's an example in which one lawyer sought to provoke another. Instead of "wrestling with the pig," Lawyer Piersall obtained a court order punishing Lawyer Talbot:

PIERSALL: ...The question is: do you have any independent recollection of what dealings a company by the name of Hydro Engineering, Inc., of which you were a principal, had with my client, Impell Corporation, in the year 1985? Do you or don't you have any independent recollection?

TALBOT: I want to know whether you have got some documents that you should have produced to us but you have refused to produce on the basis of some kind of dilatory objection to our request for documents that has been outstanding for a long time? What's the answer to my question, Piersall?

PIERSALL: I'm not being deposed, Mr. Talbot.

TALBOT: Well, then, I'm going to instruct the witness, until you satisfy our document request, that he need not answer a question related to a document which you should have produced to us.

PIERSALL: Do you refuse to answer my last question, Mr. McPeak?

TALBOT: He doesn't need to say anything to you, Piersall. Move on.

PIERSALL: Excuse me, I would suggest —

TALBOT: You're excused.

PIERSALL: — that you either refer to me as Mr. Piersall or Jeff.

TALBOT: It's going to be Piersall.

PIERSALL: Well —

TALBOT: You know why? Because that affidavit that I saw that you filed up in Washington is a lie.

PIERSALL: No it's not.

TALBOT: *And I'm calling you a liar, Piersall.*

PIERSALL: *Well, you call me whatever you like.*

TALBOT: *You're a —*

PIERSALL: *And the judge will consider what your activities are in this deposition.*

TALBOT: *You're a liar, Piersall. Aren't you going to be a man and do something about it?*

PIERSALL: *Mr. McPeak, do you refuse to answer my last question?*

TALBOT: *He doesn't need to answer you, Piersall.*

PIERSALL: *Okay. You're instructing him not to?*

TALBOT: *We're instructing him not to, Piersall. You got any more questions, liar?*

PIERSALL: *That's the end of this deposition. We'll be moving for sanctions against you.*

TALBOT: *Let's go on with the deposition.*

PIERSALL: *No, sir, not with this conduct going on. I'll be moving for a grievance against you, too, Irv.*

TALBOT: *Do it.*

PIERSALL: *You bet. You got it. Let me just note on the record, this deposition is being recessed until the court can hear a motion that we'll be filing designed to have Mr. Talbot control himself during the conduct of depositions.*

> *Mr. McPeak, I'm sorry for any inconvenience to you in having to resume this deposition at a later date.*

TALBOT: *He's not going to have to resume it. We're here to answer questions.*

> *I'll tell you what I'll do, Piersall. I'll leave the room and you can continue the deposition.*

PIERSALL: *That would be great.*

TALBOT: *I hope it's not. I'm going to take your deposition about that affidavit.*

PIERSALL: *You just do whatever you can.*

TALBOT: *I noticed your lawyer in Austin didn't think enough of it to file it in this case once I talked with him about it. And if you ever want to do something about what I said to you, I'll be glad to.*

PIERSALL: *I've already told you that I plan to do it. I plan to file a motion for sanctions against you and I plan to file a grievance against you.*

TALBOT: Good.
PIERSALL: Note for the record that Mr. Talbot has left the room
and we're going to try to proceed with the deposition.

Mr. Piersall did not take the bait. In fact, he filed the motion for sanctions that he promised and succeeded in barring Mr. Talbot from appearing further in the case. The difference between the behavior of both sides in previous examples and that of Mr. Piersall is significant in that Piersall was aggressive without being hostile. Aggressive conduct is conduct that, while it may be opposed to the interests of another, serves appropriate objectives. Hostile conduct, on the other hand, has just one purpose: to prevail over or injure another. Piersall's objective was simply to get the opposing lawyer, who had lost self-control, out of the lawsuit so that the parties could proceed to resolve the conflict.

We have seen now that the legal system teaches two responses to provocation: (1) a response in kind, and (2) an appeal to a third-party decision-maker. This pattern begins with clients who, unable to resolve their own disputes, either respond in kind to opposing parties or seek the intervention of an adjudicator. Similarly, lawyers are programmed to either respond in kind or seek the intervention of a neutral party (i.e., a judge).

Whether we respond in kind or appeal to a third party, our modus operandi is *justification* and *blaming*. Note that even Mr. Piersall, who was acting appropriately in getting third-party help, did not seek to determine his own responsibility for triggering the admittedly inappropriate outburst from Talbot. Instead, he went to court, as would any competent lawyer operating within the traditional rules of the civil-justice system, and convinced the judge that the blame for the altercation should fall on Talbot.

Although Mr. Piersall obtained a happy interim result, conflicts resolved in the midst of justifying and blaming typically produce unsatisfying results in the end. If the case is adjudicated, whether by an arbitrator, a judge, or a jury, the "losing" side is guaranteed to be unhappy because of the result and the cost. The "winning" side, too, will probably be less than happy because of the additional cost and delay, not to mention, as is likely, the result being one that's short of a total victory.

Let me cite, as examples, two cases that I tried in the same year, each time winning six-figure verdicts.

The first was a homeowners' suit against a manufacturing company that had supplied some defective building products. The company decision-maker, a Mr. Macho, offered very little to settle, believing that the company could win on a technicality. He was proved wrong; we won a judgment of over $200,000. If you add the company's attorney's fees to the amount of the judgment, the total comes to over three times what my clients would have accepted to settle early. But are they enjoying their victory? Hardly. They have yet to see a dime from the judgment, though they've spent over $50,000 in litigation costs alone (none of which were fees to me). So what happened? The company appealed the judgment—and, while the appeal was pending, filed bankruptcy. Although we were mostly successful on the appeal, the case today, nine years later, remains captive of a so-called Chapter 11 "reorganization"—in theory, it's a way for a corporation to stave off creditors until it can "reorganize" to pay its debts. In practice, it's a travesty.

The second case involved an architectural firm (my client) suing a rival firm over some lost fees. The rival firm had promised to split a fee with my client and then reneged on the promise; it also refused to make any settlement offer. After hearing the evidence, the jury awarded my client over $400,000 and found that the defendant firm had committed fraud. But the judgment we took put the defendant firm in bankruptcy, and it soon broke up. Consequently, my client never collected a penny.

The unhappy results of these cases are only two examples of the widespread dissatisfaction among participants in litigation. In a consumer survey, lawyers hired to handle adversarial matters had the second worst all-time ranking of 27% customer dissatisfaction, better only than diet plans ("When You Need a Lawyer" 34). True, the other side of this statistic is that 73% of our customers may be satisfied. But even when the early results appear favorable, the end results may be disappointing. I have personally handled many cases for plaintiffs in which we obtained judgments for many times the amount we would have taken had the cases settled early. That was the good news. The bad news was that the clients had to wait many months and sometimes years to recover, and they and the defendants had residual rancor from the process. On the other hand, just recently I mediated a case in which the plaintiffs were offered far more than I thought the case was worth. The plaintiffs and their lawyer turned it down. Within a week a trial judge gave them nothing. An appeal will surely follow and be costly to the victorious defendant. No one will be happy, whatever the result.

This is not to suggest that people shouldn't hire lawyers or that people are not better off after hiring lawyers than they would have been if they hadn't. The fact is, lawyers are essential to even the playing field when someone faces a powerful opponent who refuses to accept responsibility for a wrong. I have represented a large number of mom-and-pop small-business owners against large companies who made misrepresentations in selling them businesses, sometimes costing them their life savings. In every case, I believe my clients fared better after the lawsuits than before. Overall, more than 90% of my clients end up better off financially than they were before taking legal action. I believe many plaintiffs' lawyers can legitimately make similar claims.

But even though we are often needed and we do improve our clients' situations, we do it at great cost. So how can we create a system that offers satisfactory results more often with lower cost? Surely there's a better way.

CHAPTER 4

DEATH
BY TEDIUM

In the Philip Morris v. ABC TV *litigation, the
cigarette giant delivered 25 boxes of documents
on "hard-to-photocopy paper, dyed dark red,
that additionally seemed to have been treated
chemically to smell foul."*
—From the *ABA Journal,* November 1995

"Death by tedium" refers to a strategy, common
among lawyers, for doing the other party in via relentless
information-gathering. The two chief means are written
discovery and depositions. Examples of each will convey
the nature of the problem.

Document Death, Deposition Death

"Written discovery" is a means of getting information
from the other side. One form of written discovery is the
"request for production," which compels your opponent
to furnish documents for inspection and copying. The
request for production begins with definitions that are
then incorporated into separate requests for documents
relating to various topics. To get a flavor for how tedious
written discovery can be, consider the following definition
contained in a recent request for production sent to me:

*"Documents": The term "documents" shall mean writings and
all other tangible things of every type and from any source,
including originals and non-identical copies thereof, that are in*

your possession, custody or control or known by you to exist.
This would include documents sent outside to any person or
source as well as documents intended for internal use.

The term also includes communications not only in words,
but in symbols, pictures, sound recordings, film, tapes, and
information stored in, or accessible through, computer or other
information storage or retrieval systems. If the information is
kept in a computer or information storage or retrieval system,
the term also includes codes and programming instructions and
other materials necessary to understand such systems.

The term includes, but is not limited to: papers, books, pho-
tographs, electronic or videotape recordings, and any other data
compilations from which information can be obtained and
translated, if necessary, by the person from whom production is
sought, into reasonably usable form, calendars, checks, agenda,
agreements, analyses, bills, invoices, records of obligations and
expenditures, correspondence, diaries, telexes, telegrams, tele-
types, cables, telefaxes, files, legal documents, financial state-
ments and documents including balance sheets and profit and
loss statements, accounting entries, letters, memorandum [sic]
recording telephone or in-person conferences or meetings or con-
versations, manuals, books, pamphlets, periodicals, articles,
press releases, purchase orders, receipts, records, handwritten
notes, schedules, contracts, agreements, studies, memos of
interviews, evaluations, written reports of tests or experiments,
laboratory records, public relations releases, workpapers, charts,
drawings, sketches, graphs, indices, lists, tapes, photographs,
microfilm or microfiche, data sheet or data process cards, drafts
of documents, accounts, drawings, graphs, charts, photographs,
electronic and videotape recordings, and any other data compi-
lations from which information can be obtained and translat-
ed, if necessary, by the person from whom production is sought,
into reasonably usable form, and all other writings whose con-
tents relate or are relevant to the subject matter of the discovery
request or that constitute or contain matters relevant to the....

Other forms of written discovery include "interrogatories," which are questions that seek written answers, and
"requests for admission," which are statements that require the opponent to admit or deny their truth. These

methods permit discovery of the other side's case so as to prepare a response. In addition, they are designed to obtain information for building one's own case. For example, in a medical malpractice case, it may be important to get the hospital's records in order to determine what the doctor knew when making certain decisions. Written discovery is also used to simplify introducing the evidence at trial. For example, we have procedures for putting medical bills into evidence at a trial without having to call a busy (and expensive) doctor to testify.

Depositions of witnesses are conducted under oath in question-and-answer form and transcribed by a court reporter. Like written discovery, they are meant for obtaining information to build one's own case and to respond adequately to the opponent's case.

Unfortunately, we use these discovery tools for other purposes as well. One purpose is to win on technicalities. In Texas, for example, courts (in the past) have prevented key witnesses from testifying simply because a lawyer forgot to list an address or update a phone number. This result has occurred even when the other side knew the whereabouts of the witness and was prepared to respond to the witness's testimony.

A second purpose is to win by attrition. Plaintiffs with long-shot cases may cause defendants to spend so much in legal fees that they're eventually compelled to settle. It can work the other way as well, of course: defendants can make a case so expensive that some plaintiffs run out of resources and have to give up by settling for far less than the case would otherwise be worth.

I once represented one of two defendants that had been sued by the same plaintiff. The other defendant was represented by a master of attrition. He said one day that he intended to take a deposition by "taking the witness back to the third grade and reliving every day of his life." When I suggested that we had a strong case and should proceed to trial, he responded, "In every case, you have at least a 30% chance of losing, but we can guarantee that he [the plaintiff's lawyer] will give up if we exhaust his resources." The master of attrition was a named partner in a firm notorious for such behavior. Other lawyers may be less brazen about such tactics, but they are common nevertheless.

A corollary tactic is to inundate the opponent. Some lawyers respond to document requests with a technique called "boxcarring." As the name implies, this technique involves responding in a literal way to a request by supplying not only the documents that one knows are being sought, but by producing everything to which the request could conceivably refer. The name probably comes from an apocryphal story about some hapless requesting lawyer who gets a call that his documents are awaiting him at the railyard—and that storage charges will begin if he doesn't remove them.

There is no end to lawyer creativity when it comes to paper wars. In the *Philip Morris v. ABC TV* litigation, the cigarette giant delivered 25 boxes of documents on "hard-to-photocopy paper, dyed dark red, that additionally seemed to have been treated chemically to smell foul" (Weinberg 103).

Death by Delay

In October 1989, less than a year after suit was filed, I obtained on behalf of my clients—101 condominium homeowners—a judgment of over $200,000. This is the same case I discussed in Chapter 3 in which the judgment remained uncollected for nine years because of a protracted bankruptcy. Although two United States Supreme Court Justices characterized the reasons relied on by the other side for delay as "frivolous," the delay continued. Ironically, my clients were relatively lucky. For more than eight years a number of asbestos victims, who had judgments against the same company totalling millions of dollars, were also delayed until they settled for discounted amounts—and many literally died in the interim.

Death by delay afflicts big companies as well. In one case, an internal corporate battle orchestrated by the company lawyer precluded sale of a major company asset, costing the majority stockholders literally billions. In another mammoth lawsuit, where an oil company sued its own insurance company for several hundred million dollars because the insurance company had allegedly refused and delayed paying a claim, the oil company was required to endure not only the original trial and all the appeals on the basic claim, but the scheduling of yet another trial—this one for damages from bad-faith conduct. The entire case was expected to take many years to complete had it not settled after the first trial.

Fear, Fear, and More Fear

I have never met a lawyer who admitted to liking paper wars. Yet, as one might expect by now, we are driven to engage in death by tedium by the same fears that lead us to engage in other repugnant behavior. The thinking is that if we don't turn over every stone, we might not find that one crucial smoking gun (if I may inelegantly mix metaphors) and might therefore be overpowered and fail.

A fear commonly associated with death by tedium is the same fear that inspires other compulsive behavior: a loss of control. Many of us feel that if we can just cover all the bases, be totally thorough, leave nothing to chance, then everything will be okay. After unsuccessful trial outings early in my career I sometimes sat there thinking, "If I had only done [blank], we would have won." It was a thought accompanied by feelings that I sought to avoid experiencing at all costs.

The Costs

Death by tedium has obvious costs. One is legal fees. These fees are unnecessarily high because, out of fear, we sometimes compulsively engage in discovery without regard to the cost or benefit to the client. Here we resemble physicians who prescribe expensive tests for fear of malpractice suits instead of from a risk/benefit analysis from the patient's standpoint. In addition, clients lose time and suffer aggravation answering burdensome interrogatories and dredging up documents.

Arbitrary results also generate some not-so-obvious costs. Those who lose on a technicality walk away feeling cheated and angry. So do those who are arbitrarily delayed. Indeed, they may themselves cheat the next time, thereby provoking additional conflict.

Even the beneficiaries of arbitrary results from technicalities or delays suffer their own costs. Often, they'll feel like they got away with something. And being rewarded for getting away with things may encourage them to break the law again. Once more, this is likely to provoke additional conflict.

CHAPTER 5

GREED

God loves lawyers. That's proven by the fact that there's greed in this world.... People don't just sit down and say, "Gee, I'm really sorry. I'm not as badly hurt as this lawyer said in the pleadings, and a little bit of money'd make me happy." I don't have clients comin' into my office and saying, "We've really screwed up. This is the worst product we ever made. Why don't you just go over there and cover 'em up with some money." It doesn't happen, so God loves us all.

—James L. Gallagher

The following articles appeared one under the other in my local newspaper on January 11, 1997:

[A]n armored truck...toppled on an overpass and rained more than $500,000 into one of Miami's poorest neighborhoods.... Witnesses reported seeing rush-hour commuters loading money bags into their cars and driving off while two Brinks workers lay bleeding.

"Some motorists, instead of rendering aid, grabbed sacks of money and drove away," said Lt. Bill Schwartz, a police spokesman. "These were people heading off to the office."

("Woman, 11-Year Old" A9)

The parents of a 9-year-old girl filed a $25.5 million lawsuit claiming their family will need therapy because of an "attack" on their daughter by a Cabbage Patch doll.... In their...civil lawsuit...the parents...said the doll gnawed the

child's hair to her scalp four days after Christmas....
The family's lawyer...said he came up with the
$25.5 million figure by estimating the doll's profits
and tripling them.

(Cabbage Patch A9)

The X Culture

Greed is valuing money excessively, sometimes even
compulsively. Although some people would see it as one
more form of repugnant behavior, like lying, getting physical, hardball, and death by tedium, I see it more as a
motive—and certainly one repugnant in itself. Its effects are
so pervasive in our culture that it demands its own chapter.

Think back to the XY Game in Chapter 1. Randy, you'll
recall, valued financial gain over honesty—over friendship,
too. Randy sought to profit at the expense of his class-
mates. Randy was greedy. Randy was also not a lawyer.

But Randy was also not all that atypical of the 70-odd
participants in the group. Many of them behaved roughly
the same way. And they were non-lawyers. Besides me,
only one other lawyer was present in that seminar.

In a national survey conducted in 1991, 64% of those
polled cited lack of wealth as the chief thing they'd
change about their lives (Patterson and Kim 53). That's
consistent with America's cultural values. The people we
admire most, it seems, are those who have the most
money and political power. I have a couple of friends
whom I rarely see, and the first thing they ask is, "Are you
making any money? Are you rich yet?"

Greed is pervasive in American business. In Matthew
Fox's *The REinvention of Work: A New Vision of Livelihood for
Our Time*, organizational psychologist Richard McKnight
laments:

> For most workers, managers, and executives I have
> worked with in the last 10 years, business organiza-
> tions are seen as cold, impersonal machines that
> take raw materials, capital, and people in one end,
> perform some transformation, process, or service,
> and produce money out the other end—or should....
> In the prevailing model, the ideal business posture

is characterized by words such as "competition,"
"aggression," and "winner." "Our business is only
about making money," one executive said to me,
"and the only way we can do that in our industry is
by keeping everybody uncertain and mean—inside
the company and outside it." (237)

Greed is certainly one common provocation of lawsuits. Consider, for example, the thousands of suits filed
under Texas's Deceptive Trade Practices Act during the past
two decades. Many of those suits alleged that people
committed deceptive acts and practices solely to achieve
monetary gain. Consider, too, asbestos manufacturers
nationwide. Though most of them knew that their products were causing fatal diseases, they failed to take correc-
tive action or compensate victims because of the costs.
Any lawyer can cite many examples from his or her own
practice in which making money was valued above taking
responsibility for a wrong.

There was a time when how we played the game was
more important than the monetary result. A rather well-
known 19th-century American lawyer once volunteered to
argue both sides of an appeal when his adversary could
not afford to stay in town until the case came up in the
Illinois Supreme Court. Here's his letter informing the
adversary of the result:

My dear Mr. Bishop:
    The Supreme Court came in on the appointed
day and I did my best to keep faith with you.
Apparently I argued your case better than my own,
for the court has just sent down a rescript in your
favor. Accept my heartiest congratulations.
                                   Very sincerely yours,
                                   A. Lincoln
                                   (Lang 52)

Unfortunately, Mr. Lincoln's honorable deed seems
anachronistic in today's world of win-at-all-costs. Audience after audience, when I have asked, "Which is more
important to our clients, whether we win or how we play

the game?", answer the former. And the underlying reason is typically that money is valued over all else.

Soon after I began working, I recall that my feelings of self-worth seemed to rise and fall with my bank balance. Although I didn't *feel* greedy, making money was a high priority, certainly higher than any spiritual concerns. My self-esteem was so tied up with money that when I was asked, "What is your net worth?" it was hard to avoid separating the answer in dollars from my worth as a person.

I was not unique in equating my self-worth with my wealth. In his best-seller *The Seven Habits of Highly Successful People*, Stephen Covey speaks of this phenomenon as a cultural reality, without even singling out lawyers (113-114)!

When it comes to greed, then, lawyers have no monopoly. Again, we merely reflect the culture in which we operate. Yet lawyers seem to be singled out for attack as icons of greed. And we certainly do our part to draw the criticism.

Billing Practices

One reason for it, surely, is our billing practices. Traditionally, we've billed clients by an hourly rate, regardless of whether we accomplished something of value for them. True, we might occasionally write off some time if we felt we'd spent it inefficiently—but our definition of inefficiency had little to do with whether the client could afford the services or whether the value conferred was worth the time spent. Even though our code of ethics requires that we consider the results obtained in figuring the bill, we've used that code more often to justify charging a premium for an unusually good result rather than to reduce the bill so as to bring it in line with a not-so-good result. Only recently have firms gone to "value billing," a practice in which the bill has a closer relation to the value conferred.

Evidence of the persistence of over-billing appeared in the Spring 1996 issue of *U.S. Business Litigation*:

> General counsel [company lawyers who frequently hire outside law firms] often cannot believe the bills they get from their law firms.... Corporate

counsel may not think they are being intentionally
cheated, but they do believe there is widespread
lack of sound business practices in law firms.
(Value for Litigation 1)

Lawyers have been notorious for padding bills. Many,
for instance, charge in minimum increments—say, three-
tenths of an hour, 18 minutes. This allows them to justify
billing 18 minutes for a two-minute phone call. I've heard
defense lawyers joke that it's a shame that there are only
48 hours in the day. Some of my friends acknowledge that
their firms require them to pad their bills to compensate
for low rates imposed by insurance companies. To their
credit, some have gotten into trouble with their firm's
management by refusing to do it. And then there's the
tired-out joke of the 40-year-old lawyer who dies and complains to St. Peter that he was taken too soon, to which St.
Peter replies, "According to your timeslips, you're 96."

The Medium of Exchange

Attacks on lawyers' greed also stem from the fact that
money is the medium of exchange in the adversary system. When clients come in wanting justice, we often
inform them that, in our system, justice can only be mea-
sured in money. And when our clients are plaintiffs, we're
also sure to apprise the juries of this same principle. It
happens to be true, alas. With rare exceptions, courts have
little power to award anything but money.

Given that money is the medium of exchange, lawyers
cannot effectively advise clients unless we convert every
shade of misery into dollar terms. What is the value of a
sore back? Of a broken hip? Of a wounded reputation? Of
a brain-damaged baby? This very process is dehumanizing
and makes us sound both callous and mercenary.

Scapegoats and Jealousy

A third reason we are perceived as greedy stems from
people's need for scapegoats. Americans have a love/hate
relationship with the wealthy and powerful. Although we
often revere them, we may want to deny our own greediness

by scapegoating others who are rich and powerful. Scape-goating originated when biblical tribes would purge them-selves of all sins by placing them symbolically on the head of a goat and sending the goat out into the wilderness. Lawyers are handy for this purpose, in part because we sometimes enjoy eye-popping financial success. Upon reading of large verdicts, particularly those obtained by my friends, I confess that I myself have been jealous. Such jealousy is prevalent.

But perhaps the biggest reason lawyers are reviled is that we constantly fight over money—and we do it in ways that devalue our country's humanistic tradition. In short, we appear to value money over people. For the sake of our clients' money, we deceive, we play hardball, and we cause immense aggravation. We justify, we blame, we lie, we literally fight—all in the name of justice. But it is only money that is at stake. And even though we lawyers do all of this "for our clients," we are the actual perpetra-tors. Given that many in our society subscribe to such Judeo-Christian principles as "Love thy neighbor," "Be honest," "Take responsibility," and "simple human kind-ness," and given that we routinely violate these pieties when money is at stake, and given what we know about scapegoating as a convenient way to unload our own sins—given all that, is it any wonder that we blame so much on "greedy lawyers"?

The Genesis of Greed: Our Old Friend Fear

Greed comes from a place of fear. Part of it is fear that without a certain level of income, we won't be able to sus-tain our comfortable existence. Another part of it stems from the flip side of a need for power—namely, the fear of feeling weak. Power and money go together, because in our society, money is the currency of power. Money talks. Money controls.

The Effects of Greed: Succumbing to Temptation

I have noticed that the larger the stakes in litigation, the more repugnant the behavior. This should not be sur-prising, for in all areas of life, the higher the stakes, the greater the temptation.

In a national survey of 2,000 adult Americans in 1991, subjects were asked, "What are you honestly willing to do for $10 million?" The answers were sobering. Fully 25% would abandon their entire family. In addition, 23% would become prostitutes for a week or more; 10% would withhold testimony and let a murderer go free; 7% would kill a stranger; 4% would have sex-change operations; and 3% percent would put their children up for adoption (Patterson and Kim 66).

The effect of high stakes is similar in litigation. I have noticed even now that whenever I am close to bringing home a large fee, I get single-minded about seeing the result through. Often I have to catch myself, lest I allow other values to be overshadowed by my own greed.

All of the lawyers I've introduced you to thus far, showing their warts, are highly successful—we handle large cases with high stakes. Successful lawyers actually aren't any less ethical than others. But, because of the "high-stakes effect," we are certainly subject to great temptation, and we're by no means immune to engaging in ordinary lying and other repugnant behavior just because of the air of respectability.

Whether we are tempted by large sums or small, it's easy to see how greed prompts much of our lying and other repugnant behavior. By definition, greed is valuing money over pretty much everything else—not least of which are honesty, cooperation, and efficient conflict resolution.

CHAPTER 6

A PANACEA?

A good deal is when both sides are unhappy.
—*Abe Sampson*

Mediation

Mediation is a process that uses a neutral person to facilitate resolving a conflict. Unlike in a trial, however, the neutral person is not a judge and does not make a decision. Rather, the mediator helps the participants discuss their positions and interests. The parties exchange information to help each other evaluate the case and then try to negotiate a settlement. What is said in the mediation may not be used against the parties outside of the mediation.

Mediation is often touted as a panacea for all that is wrong with the litigation system. Well, it certainly saves costs of litigation, both for the parties and for us taxpayers. But let's explore whether it is fundamentally any different from litigation in the effect it has on the parties.

Even mediation of most civil lawsuits[20] involves justifying and blaming. The parties begin with opening statements in which they try to show both the mediator and the opposition why their own position is justified or why the opposition is to blame. The mediator then tries to soften the parties' attachment to their respective positions, not by asking them to acknowledge any responsibility, but by exposing their weaknesses. Newly defensive now, both parties naturally rejustify their positions and blame the other side afresh. What then typically occurs is a contest

[20] There are several different mediation models. Some of these models actually encourage the parties to end conflict in ways that bring them closer together. However, as we'll see, these models are not typically used in the resolution of lawsuits.

of wills in which both sides exchange multiple offers, tit-for-tat, before exhaustedly reaching a settlement. A good settlement, according to the conventional wisdom of mediators, is one about which both sides are unhappy.

Here's an example of a typical mediation:

Emma Wheeler is a 24-year-old college student whose car was rear-ended twice within six months. In both accidents, she sustained neck injuries. She has brought suit against the two drivers. The parties are participating in a mediation required by the court to encourage settlement and as a prerequisite to going to trial. At the mediation are several people: the mediator, a lawyer and an insurance adjuster for each of the insurance companies of the defendant-drivers, and Emma and I, her attorney.

The insurance companies have made a combined offer to settle for $7,000 before mediation, but I speculate they have come to the mediation ready to pay $15,000. My goal is to get them to pay as much above that as I can. We need to settle this case because the cost of hiring expert witnesses, including doctors, is so high that even if we were to win a verdict of $30,000, Emma would not come out much better. I have just this week tried another injury case in which the jury awarded only $2,000 for pain and suffering to a woman who now carries three screws in her arm due to a broken elbow. The public outcry against "lawsuit abuse" has made it difficult to get much money for intangible damages like pain and suffering and physical impairment.

The Mediator: *Hello, my name is Dick Rutledge. As you know, I will be your mediator today. You have seen my resumé so I won't dwell on my background and qualifications. As you know, mediation is a process during which I attempt to facilitate a settlement. I am not a judge and I make no decision. If you want my opinion of what the case is worth, I may provide it, but only late in the game. We will begin with each side giving an opening statement and then I will separate the plaintiff's group into one room and the defendants' group into another. I will then go back and forth, similar to "shuttle diplomacy," in* *order to help you resolve this case. As you know, everything that is said in the mediation is confidential. Not only that, nothing that anyone tells me in the separate caucuses will be disclosed unless I first get your permission.*

I believe in the mediation process. It saves costs and gives you the opportunity to take control of the resolution of your problem.

We may reach an impasse in the negotiations. I will try to get past the impasse in order to resolve this case. In order to ensure that all possibilities are exhausted, I would like your agreement to continue to negotiate until I tell you that I think it's fruitless. Will everyone agree? [Everyone nods.]

I would also like to ask if anyone here will have to make any calls to obtain authority to settle. [Everyone nods "no."] *Good. Let's begin with opening statements. Mr. Perlmutter....*

MP: *This is a case of clear liability. Both defendants were negligent, and there's no dispute about that. The only question is, "How much of her damages are attributable to each collision?" The evidence we present at trial will show that although Emma had some problems with her neck before the first collision, they were mostly resolved. She was doing aerobics and pretty much living a normal life. Following the first collision, she was in significant pain but could not afford treatment, so she did not go to the doctor. She did finally hire our firm after the second collision and we arranged to have her seen by a doctor. Since then, she has incurred $8,000 in medical bills. She has also lost $1,200 in income from her job as a professional art model. She still has problems with her neck and we anticipate that she will continue to have the problems for a long time. Before mediation, the defendants offered a total of $7,000 and we countered at $35,000.*

Bill Wright: *I represent Maizie Whitcomb, who, as you know, was the driver of the first car. While we don't concede liability and will have something to say about that at trial, we are here to try to negotiate a fair settlement. However, we believe that Ms. Wheeler had neck problems before this incident. In addition, she failed to go to the doctor before the second accident. So we think she was essentially not hurt from the first accident that my client was involved in, and all her problems were caused by the pre-existing conditions and possibly aggravated by the second accident.*

Joe Campion: *Our position is that Ms. Wheeler was not significantly injured in the collision with my client. There was very little damage to either vehicle. As to her lost wages, we don't see anything in the medical records to suggest that she couldn't perform her job as a nude model. So we dispute the lost wages and feel that the medical bills were incurred in part because of the pre-existing injury and the first collision.*

The Mediator: *Would anyone else like to say anything?*

Dead silence follows, for each party has been warned by a lawyer not to say anything at this point. Even though nothing in the mediation can be repeated elsewhere, the other side still hears it and may be able to find a way to use it if the case doesn't settle.

The Mediator: *Very well. I'd like to take the defendant group into another room and talk to them first.*

At this point, we break out our reading materials. I always advise my clients to bring along reading materials to lessen the boredom while the mediator is caucusing with the opposition. This advice has the added benefit of allowing me to work on other cases or go through my mail during the mediation.[21]

(Knock at the door.)

The Mediator: *Well, I have a total of $10,000. But before you respond, I would like to hear what you think your strengths and weaknesses are.*

At this point, the wary lawyer knows that the mediator is getting information to gain concessions in his negotiating position. Therefore, he is careful to give the mediator a plausible but nonetheless rosy picture of the case.

MP: *Well, I think my client is a strength. She is obviously attractive, is working her way through school, and is just a nice person. Our weaknesses are that she had those other neck problems and, of course, they will be chicken-shit about her modeling. At the deposition, for example, you would have thought that the term "model" was found under "N" in the dictionary*

---

[21] Some of us may be tempted to bill our time in mediation to both the client for whom we are mediating and the other clients on whose matters we are working during the caucuses. In my case, since the cases I handle are almost all contingent-fee cases, I fortunately do not have to deal with that temptation.

—"nudemodeling" this and "nudemodeling" that. Of course, we do have the problem of the prior medical records in which she complains of neck problems, and Emma didn't remember some of those appointments during her deposition. You know what they'll do with that at trial.

(There is no sense in failing to mention all the negatives. The mediator will hear of them from the defense anyway. Telling him first inoculates him because I can put my spin on them.)

The Mediator: *Ms. Wheeler, do you know what he is saying?*

Ms. Wheeler: *No.*

The Mediator: *Well, the opposition will use the fact that you did not remember that you told your doctors before the collisions in this case about neck problems to suggest that you were trying to hide the previous problems. Now, I know that you weren't trying to do that, but they will try to make it look like you were.*

Ms. Wheeler: Well, *I wasn't trying to hide anything. I just forgot.*

The Mediator: *Mark, how do you evaluate this case?*

Here again, I must be careful. Some mediators keep a scorecard on the percentage of cases they settle. Since it doesn't matter to them what the settlement is as long as it settles, they will work hard on any party who shows weakness to narrow the gap between the parties. With this particular mediator, I am not worried about that, but I do not want to give him any reason to perceive any weakness of our will and unconsciously communicate it to the other side.

MP: *I think we'll get the medical and the lost wages. In addition, I think we'll get ten to twenty thousand in lost physical impairment and pain and mental anguish. Emma is young and has a long life of pain ahead of her. Her activities will be limited. She won't be able to lift heavy objects, may have problems just sitting at a desk or computer, etc.*

The Mediator: *Very well. Mark, what number do you want me to take back?*

MP: *Tell 'em $29,000. She couldn't hold still to model. They know that you can't stay in one place with a sore neck. Tell 'em, also, that that is a significant move and that we expect one in return. We don't mind being the first to get these* *discussions within the range that we think is realistic, but we need them to reciprocate.*

This particular client is willing to settle for whatever I think the case is really worth. Nevertheless, the mediator and I check with her to be sure she is comfortable with the offer. She says that she is.

At this point, the mediator leaves and we continue our work on other matters. A half-hour later, the mediator returns.

The Mediator: *They're offering $12,500. They also wanted me to show these records that they just got from the college Health Center for the period between the first and second accident.*

I look at the records. They show that my client visited the Health Center for bladder infections, colds and flu, and an abortion during this time. There is no mention of the neck problems. I show the records to my client.

Ms. Wheeler: *I can't believe that they got those records! I am freaking out! How dare they invade my privacy like that!*

The Mediator: *Unfortunately, litigation is blood sport.*

MP: *Emma, I agree that it is outrageous that they would have access to those records and learn so much about your personal life. You have every right to feel both outrage and hurt. I'm sorry that you're having to go through this brutal process. How are you doing?*

Ms. Wheeler: *I'm just going to have to go home and be around people who care about me tonight. This is just horrible! I just don't know what to say!*

MP: *Do you feel okay about continuing now?*

Ms. Wheeler: *Yeah, I guess.*

MP: *Can you tell me why you didn't say anything about the neck problems to the people at the Health Center?*

Ms. Wheeler: *Sure! They don't have neurologists, chiropractors, and physical therapists there. I didn't think they could help me.*

MP: *I understand, but we are still going to have a problem with this. People on juries these days are highly suspicious, and the other side will be able to raise some doubt, even though I believe you. I think we ought to counter $26,000. Tell them that she didn't believe that the Health Center treated this kind of problem.*

At this point, the mediator leaves. Presently he returns and says that the insurance company offers $14,000. He also says to Emma, *"By the way, of course, they want you to know that they're sorry you were hurt."* The apology may be sincere, but everyone hears it as if it is conveyed with lawyerly sincerity. I mutter something like *"...as if an insurance company can have a heart from which to apologize."*

I respond "$24,000" and send the mediator on his way. They then come back with $15,000. I say that if they would make an offer of $20,000, we would accept it. They counter with $16,000. We say $19,400, to which they say $17,000. Finally, we settle on $17,550, the $550 representing the court costs. On refusing my last attempt to wangle a little more money out of the insurance company, one adjuster testily remarks that the companies have already paid substantially more than they had intended. The mediator says that they had been behaving like $15,000 was a hard "bottom line" and highly resent paying more than they feel the case is worth. After paying her medical bills and litigation expenses, the client is left with just $1,000 even after we cut our fee.

Let's examine the messages with which the parties leave such a mediation. My client was essentially told that it's necessary to *force* other people to take responsibility for wrongs. After such an experience, the internal message that is likely to guide her life is, "Why should I voluntarily take responsibility for anything that I do when others don't?"

Emma was also told that the mere act of attempting to stand up for her rights will subject her to embarrassing personal attacks and invasions of her privacy. Despite the mediator's valiant efforts to make her feel better, she left feeling violated and angry. People subjected to such treatment will tend either to flee a similar situation or to fight with stridency. Both strategies are neither consistent with her assuming personal responsibility nor apt to encourage those with whom she comes into conflict to take personal responsibility.

The insurance companies, meanwhile, were told that plaintiffs bring questionable claims, and that the companies must protect their dollars from such specious claims with hard bargaining. They will continue to be suspicious of future claimants and will resist being overpowered. These strategies also do not embrace the assumption of personal responsibility.

Most mediators would consider Emma Wheeler's mediation successful. Why? Ironically, because it reached a settlement that left both sides unhappy, thus proving it was fair! And, certainly, it saved the cost of further litigation. But when we consider how many Emma Wheelers there are and how many experience the legal system as a sausage grinder, it's no wonder that the legal system feeds the beast of competitive justify/blame interactions. No wonder we fear one another.

Responsibility

Occasionally in mediations, a party will acknowledge some responsibility for provoking the conflict. When this happens, it opens the door for both parties to walk out of the mediation pleased with the result and with internal messages that encourage responsible conflict resolution. Let's look at an example—a case involving a dispute over a shopping-mall lease.

———————

One day, Don, the mall owner, paid a visit to Robert, manager of Harvey's Sporting Goods. The store had been selling sporting-event tickets. Don was concerned that the mall would incur liability from another business that had the exclusive right under its lease to sell sporting-event tickets in the mall.

After a brief introduction, Don curtly told Robert, *"I can't have you selling sporting-event tickets here when Ticket Vendors has an exclusive right to sell tickets in the mall. If you don't stop immediately, we'll have to terminate your lease."*

Harvey's had a lease with a very low rent, considering the current market. Knowing this, Robert figured that Don's complaint was just an excuse to terminate the lease and get a higher rent. He shot back, *"Why don't you get out of here? We don't need any help running our business! There's nothing in our lease that prevents us from selling tickets. This is not our problem."*

Don's last words as he left the store were, *"[I]f you want to fight, well, we know how to fight!"*

The mall then filed suit to terminate Harvey's Sporting Goods' lease. At a hearing, Harvey's sought to stop the action. The judge then referred the case to mediation.

When I began conducting the mediation, the parties assured me that Don and Robert, who were both at the mediation, had full authority to enter into a settlement. But after a day of mediation it became clear that the key player for Harvey's was not the manager, Robert, but the owner, Harvey. It also became clear that Don and Robert's incompatible communication styles were more significant in precipitating the litigation than substantive issues. Upon speaking to Harvey, I felt that his style was more compatible with Don than Robert's, so I suggested that they talk. First, though, I wanted Don to acknowledge some responsibility for provoking the fight and to begin the conversation with a sincere apology. So I explained why I thought the conflict began, and he agreed that he could have handled it better. The conversation went this way:

MP: *Harvey, I have Don in here on the speaker phone and I thought that it would be most productive if the two of you talked, person to person, without any intermediaries. Everyone here, including the lawyers, has agreed that would be okay with them, so, without any further delay, I want to introduce Don Marshall, who is the owner of the shopping center.*

DON: *Harvey, my name is Don, and I want to tell you that I'm sorry that we didn't get a chance to talk a little earlier because, if we had, maybe things wouldn't have gotten to this point. But, if I may, I'd like to tell you a little bit about what my side wants and then afford you the courtesy of doing the same for you. I own shopping centers in several states and two foreign countries. My business is running shopping centers. If I have to yell into the phone to make this clear, I will do it, but I want you to know that we are not, I repeat not, interested in coming in here and simply busting the lease. We came in and found that you were selling tickets and were upset about it. We took an*

*aggressive posture, and I apologize for that. We hoped to get some-
one's attention, and maybe that wasn't the best way to do it.*

*Our objective is to make money with the center, to add
value to it. We can do that if you are successful and if we can
keep our obligations to our other tenants. We would like to
work with you any way we can to ensure your success. We've
got some plans that we'll be happy to send to you in advance as
to what we are doing with the mall. We would like to work
with you in any way we can to find a way to make this a win
for both of us. We have some plans to improve the center and
would like to help you in your business in any way that we can.
Now that I've spent a little time telling you where we're coming
from, I'd like to afford you the courtesy to do the same.*

HARVEY: *Well, let's talk.*

Harvey and Don then exchanged ideas about when
they'd meet to develop a business solution to the conflict.
The lawyers agreed to postpone any further litigation
pending the discussions between the parties. The case
then settled without further litigation.

What happened between Don and Harvey illustrates a
critical choice. Both parties took back from their lawyers
and from the mediator the responsibility for resolving the
dispute. They were not able to do this successfully until
one party *unconditionally acknowledged responsibility* for initially provoking the conflict. So long as both sides were
justifying and blaming, they were moving headlong into
an expensive, wasteful, and unsatisfying process. This
result is consistent with my experience that when a party
who initially provoked a conflict unconditionally takes
responsibility for his or her conduct, a resolution with
which *both* parties are satisfied can be obtained.

There are two important lessons from this discussion
of mediation. First, so long as parties operate from their
fears—justifying themselves and blaming the opposition—
the result is likely to be both unsatisfying and destructive
on the parties' attitude toward resolving future conflicts.
Second, regardless of the context (in this case, mediation),
a party always has the choice of justifying, blaming, and
competing, or of taking responsibility and shifting to a
cooperative mode.

Creeds and Rules

One effort to encourage lawyers to avoid hostility has been the adoption of professional creeds in many states.[22] Like the Texas Lawyers Creed, they all encourage lawyers to be civil, honest, and responsible. The Texas Lawyers Creed went into effect in November 1989. Shortly thereafter, I asked audiences of lawyers, "How many of you know that the Texas Lawyers Creed went into effect last November?" Usually, a smattering of hands would go up. I would then ask, "How many of you have noticed a marked change in lawyer behavior since that time?" Predictably, no one raised a hand.

In all fairness to the Texas creed, I believe that it's had several salutary effects, although it falls far short of eliminating lying and other repugnant behavior. First, it has set a standard and thereby a suggested cultural norm. This at least gives legitimacy to being civil; theoretically, one can be civil and not be perceived as being weak. Second, it also helps reduce the fear of malpractice suits from being less than totally hostile by setting an acceptable standard of conduct. Finally, it has somewhat reduced the number of "discovery fights" and other uncivil behavior as lawyers have become more familiar with the dictates of the creed.

Wisely, these creeds are aspirational. That is, they provide a standard for laudatory behavior without providing sanctions for falling short. The rules of disciplinary conduct and the rules of civil procedure of course already provide consequences for falling short of the standard that they set, but such enforceable rules have proved no solution because of lawyers' tendency to see them as simply the outer limits of a response to a provocation. For example, in the mid-'80s, courts and rulemakers promulgated various sanctions—payment of fines, payment of the opposition's attorney fees, even, in extreme cases, losing by default to discourage discovery abuse. But instead of reducing the amount of uncivil conflict, this remedy set off a whole new round of abuse of the sanction practice.

[22] As of 1996, at least 17 states, including Texas, Kentucky, Massachusetts, Mississippi, Montana, and Virginia, had adopted professionalism creeds.

In response, some law firms instituted internal "sanction committees" that reviewed all motions for sanction to prevent a provoked firm member from abusing the motion for sanctions in angry retaliation.

As laudatory as the professionalism creeds are in intent, however, they have left much work to be done. Hardball continues; even knowing where the line is between propriety and incivility, virtually all of us cross it from time to time. And, as we have seen, we do it because *the adversary system, the fundamental assumption of which requires our using every available means to prevail, invariably pushes lawyers to the edge of propriety*. It engenders provocation-and-response behavior that tends to escalate, and is perpetrated by people who are conditioned to rationalize whatever we do by justifying and blaming, and who are acting on subconscious fears and making unconscious choices. Is it any wonder that we often fall into the abyss of deception and hostility?

Legislation

Driven by business and insurance interests, legislators have made numerous efforts recently, at both the state and federal level, to change the civil-justice system. Under the heading of "tort reform," these efforts invariably shift the balance of power in favor of defendants at the expense of plaintiffs. In fact, between 1988 and 1994, there was a steady decline in the number of civil suits filed in American state courts from 16 million to just over 14 million, due in part to tort-reform efforts eliminating or reducing the attractiveness of civil remedies (White 203-204; "Review on the Litigation Explosion" 1).

One example of such a reform measure is the contingent-fee limit. Most plaintiff's lawyers, of which I am one, expect to be paid a percentage of the recovery (usually from 33%-40%) and are owed nothing by the client if we are unsuccessful, whereas defense lawyers are typically paid hourly fees, win or lose. Seeking to decrease the incentives for plaintiff's lawyers to take cases, reformers have promulgated legislation to eliminate or cut the percentages of contingent fees.

A second example is limits on joint and several liability. "Joint and several liability" occurs when a party's conduct is a partial cause of the occurrence giving rise to the plaintiff's injuries. Traditionally, such a party might have had to pay for all of the damages if the other responsible parties were insolvent—even if the solvent party's conduct was only a minor cause of the injuries. Limits on joint and several liability require, for example, that one must be at least a certain percent—say, 50%—responsible before joint and several will apply.

A third example is increasing the standard or burden of proof. Defense-oriented interests have made many attempts to increase the burden of proof that a plaintiff must meet in order to win. Traditionally, a plaintiff must show that the defendant was negligent—that he or she failed to use the care of an ordinarily prudent person under the same or similar circumstances. As a result of tort reforms, in certain types of cases, plaintiffs must now prove gross negligence in order to recover anything. Gross negligence requires not only ordinary negligence but also a showing of an actual conscious disregard of the plaintiff's rights. There have also been efforts to change the burden of proof from a "preponderance of the evidence," which means the greater weight of the credible evidence, to a "clear and convincing" burden.

Another example of a "tort reform" is punitive damage caps. In cases where the defendant's conduct is particularly outrageous, juries have often awarded punitive damages in order to deter future conduct or to punish past behavior. Punitive damage caps limit the amount of such damages that juries can award.

In addition, there have been calls for reform in the way we select our judges, in class-action procedures, and in consumer-protection laws. These are among countless recent attempts to shift the balance of power toward defendants.

To add a little perspective, reform efforts were moving in the opposite direction in the early '70s. Whereas today the perceived evil is increasing product and insurance costs because of "too many lawsuits," the perceived evil in the early '70s was that there were too many deserving injury victims going uncompensated. At that time, in many states, if the plaintiff was even 1% responsible for his or her own injuries and the defendant was 99% responsible, the defendant went free and the plaintiff went uncompensated.

Although, as a plaintiff's lawyer, I have my own feelings about the merits of "tort reform," they are not relevant here. What is relevant is that while such efforts may curb some of the more outrageous abuses of the system, they fail to address the true underlying sickness in it. Whether we are for or against "tort reform," we are just playing out the same dynamics that characterize the civil-justice system at its worst. The "pro's" play on our fears of high insurance rates and product costs, while the "anti's" play on our fears of victimization by powerful adversaries. Each group blames the other and justifies its own conduct. Billions are spent on lobbyists and campaign contributions, all in efforts by each side to overpower the other. Instinctively, we know that this money-driven, see-saw battle is as insane a way to make policy as the similar battle in the justice system is to resolve conflict. Yet, this see-saw battle has been waged non-stop for more years than anyone wants to remember.

These battles both in politics and in the legal system are all about who gets what. There will always be a need for rules governing such battles—and room for improved fairness in those rules. Yet there is precious little constructive effort directed to the fundamentals of *how* we decide. Could the way we fight be as important as the results we fight for? Should we continue to make decisions based solely on who can overpower whom? Are there ways that we can lessen the enormous costs, both economic and social, of unproductive conflict? These questions, among others, we address in Parts II and III.

CHAPTER 7

THE WINDS OF REVOLUTION

A revolution is poised to surge through our legal system. Its seeds lie within the legal system itself. As combatants inexorably increase their capabilities to destroy one another, the price of both victory and defeat escalates. But that paradoxically produces the inevitability of peace. Just as the advent of nuclear weapons fostered détente, the powerful new weapons of litigation—video recreations, computer animations, computer-aided research, on-line services, experts on everything, focus groups, jury consultants—are ushering in a new order.

The escalated conflict in our legal arena coincides with the increased sense of human disconnection and alienation in American society at large. The plethora of lawsuits today proves that people have become more conditioned to file suit than to pursue amicable resolution. The gross incivility in politics is another example of disaffection. The worse these problems become, the more we yearn for peace.

A deep, increasingly urgent societal yearning for peace and connection helps explain the popularity of best-sellers like *The Seven Habits of Highly Effective People* (Covey), advocating win/win thinking and human understanding; and *A Return to Love* (Williamson), advocating the displacement of fear with love. Calls for civility from political-interest groups and voter antipathy toward negative campaigning are still more evidence of a revolution in our thinking. So, too, is the complete rethinking of work in business and other spheres, as in *The REinvention of Work* (Fox), *Spirit at Work* (Conger, *et al.*), *Corporate Renaissance* (Osterberg), and *Community Building: Renewing Spirit &*

Learning in Business (Gozdz). Even lawyers are writing revolutionary manifestos in such inspiring works as *In Search of Atticus Finch* (Papantonio) and *The Soul of the Law* (Sells).

The revolution in our civil-justice system began with the lawyer creeds and court initiatives in the late '80s under the rubric of "professionalism." It accelerated in the early '90s with the mediation movement that took hold in many parts of the country. Revolution in the justice system stands poised for even more rapid acceleration with the advent of a few lawyers who have gone into the business of managing cases for companies with high volumes of litigation to facilitate their rapid and efficient resolution. These case-management specialists ride herd on the trial lawyers to ensure that the cases are settled quickly and economically.

From the outside, the revolution presses in on a resistant civil-justice system like the weight of the ocean on a steel-clad submarine. Direct pressure comes from cost-conscious, large-business litigants who see their cases pragmatically as problems to be solved rather than cases to be tried. It comes from heavyweight institutional clients who, with increasing frequency, require competitive bids for legal representation and insist on "alternative billing methods"—contingent fees, flat fees, and capped fees. It comes from divorcing spouses who recognize the insanity of hostility and seek peace for their children and themselves. It comes from "partnering" efforts such as those in the construction industry. Initiated by Lester Edelman, Chief Counsel for the Army Corps of Engineers, such innovative techniques to *prevent* disputes and resolve those that do occur without litigation have reduced the Corps' contract-claims caseload fully 71% and reduced "transaction costs" from equal-employment-opportunity complaints by a whopping 80%.[23] The Corps' dispute-prevention and -resolution techniques are rapidly spreading into the private sector.

While these outside influences pressure the civil-justice system, this revolution truly begins inside all of us

---

[23] My source is a telephone conversation with Lester Edelman in 1996.

as we seek to become *conscious* of our present reality and to take responsibility for contributing to problems rather than blaming others. When we make this internal journey, we learn that *our ability to avoid unproductive conflict hinges on our ability to choose courage over fear.* I'll explain how we can actually choose something that may appear to be a matter of character in the introduction to Part III.

With the advance of the revolution, we begin to courageously choose the pursuit of peace and take personal responsibility for our own contributions to unproductive conflict. As business people, civic and political leaders, religious leaders, lovers and friends, and even as divorcing spouses, we lead by example. The power of our integrity causes others to want to emulate us. As more and more of us transform our way of being, who we are now will be reflected in our systems.

In the civil-justice system, the results will be: (1) people will settle more disputes without needing either third-party mediators or litigation; (2) cases that do proceed to litigation will settle earlier and at much lower cost; and (3) everyone involved will enjoy a much higher satisfaction level with the outcome of the dispute-resolution process.

The revolution will have dramatic economic consequences as well. Imagine, for example, how productive our country will be when the partnering techniques of the construction industry become standard operating procedure. Imagine the life of the traditional litigator when, as a result, 70%–80% of litigation revenues disappear. Although significant dislocation will occur, the revolution does not necessarily mean massive unemployment for the legal profession, but it will certainly require a new conception of what it means to be a lawyer. The cover of the *American Bar Association Journal* for August 1996 bore these prescient words:

> The Lawyer Turns Peacemaker...As adversaries turn from litigation to mediation to resolve differences, the future will belong to attorneys who can lead the way to common ground....

No longer will being a lawyer merely mean preparing and trying cases; it will mean resolving conflict. Lawyers will need to be able to prevent war, to make war, and to shift rapidly to peace-making once it starts. These skills will enable lawyers to develop a new practice specialty that I'm calling "pre-dispute resolution" that will enable them to train people to prevent and resolve their own disputes. In the following chapters, I present a collection of principles for preventing and resolving unproductive conflict. I call it "Centered Conflict Resolution™." Learning and implementing these principles will enable lawyers to help others avoid the kind of conflict that produces lawsuits, and to expeditiously resolve whatever conflicts do arise. Such services will have great value, considering the exorbitant emotional and monetary cost of litigation.

If we make the legal system one that effectively resolves problems in this way, more people will be attracted to it; more people will seek the services of lawyers to empower them to resolve their disputes productively. Instead of milking relatively few lawsuits, successful lawyers will earn the same fees by resolving many disputes.

But for this systemic transformation to occur, there must be personal transformation. I do not mean the learning of a new set of skills, although an awareness of skills may be helpful in achieving it. Instead, I mean changing in a way that goes to the core of one's being. It entails embracing and internalizing a set of principles that govern how we see ourselves and other people. Once internalized, these principles will enable us to engage in Centered Conflict Resolution rather than lying and other repugnant behavior.

This internal *transformation* will be my focus for the remainder of the book. Part II, "Consciousness," explains how we can discover where we are in relationship to ourselves, to others, and to the universe itself; and Part III, "Courage," describes a place we can go if we choose. Mastery of the principles contained in the following chapters will help anyone, not just lawyers, to avoid unproductive conflict: parents and children, spouses (whether intending to stay married or not), people in intimate relationships, people in formerly intimate relationships, business people, civic and religious leaders . . .

PART II

CONSCIOUSNESS

INTRODUCTION
TO PART II

Several friends of mine, reviewing early drafts of this book, asked me, "Were you really that bad?" and "What caused you to change?" My unflinching answer to the first question was, "Yes, I really did those things," but answering their second question was not so easy.

Fortunately, I never had to "bottom out" like many alcoholics, who must lose their lives before getting sober, or like political criminals who find religion only in prison. Even during my lying days, I enjoyed a pretty good reputation and I had solid professional credentials.

I never even really "got caught." Although I'm sure a few lawyers saw through my deception, for the most part they were too polite to call me on it; others probably did not notice it because it wasn't out of the ordinary. In fact, when I recently attempted to apologize to one lawyer for having lied during a trial with him, he had absolutely no recollection of it. Although it's possible that he wasn't listening while I lied, I rather believe it was the kind of lie that was so commonplace for a lawyer that it did not particularly stand out to him.[24] In short, the direct consequences of lying and other repugnant behavior were not intolerable for me.

What caused me to begin to change was something more subtle. It wasn't that I had lain awake in anguish and guilt. Nor did I attend some mind-blowing workshop or suddenly find the secret of life. In the wake of some personal

[24] While he didn't remember my lying, he did remember that I had belittled him during final argument by sarcastically commenting on his "blazing cross-examination" of my expert witness. I mention this incident not only to illustrate how commonplace and expected lying is in the legal profession, but also to note how deeply hostility touches other people—in my case, often without my even knowing it.

failures, which I'll discuss presently, I simply began to be more conscious of what was going on around me. I noticed little things. There were inconsistencies in my beliefs and my actions—like giving a speech on ethics one week and then, a week later, lying during a settlement negotiation. I also became more conscious of how people reacted to me. I would joke with an opposing lawyer, who'd then turn defensive or hostile, and I'd realize that my jokes had an edge to them. I noticed feelings that I had—anger, for example, or a tightness in my lower back when I'd get back in my car at day's end. I began to notice that I was guilty of many things for which I criticized others.

I suspect that I would not have been open to such self-examination had it not been for the experience of great failure in my life and the self-examination that such failure stimulated. (I consider my greatest failures in the traditional sense of the word to be my two marriages, both of which ended in divorce.) I have known many people who've been spared significant tragedy or failure, whose lives seem to be working pretty well and who never appear to have occasion to dig deeply inside. I have known others who have experienced considerable tragedy or failure and yet, for some reason, also do not look inwardly. Part of me envies those who have not had the opportunities for growth that I have had. On the other hand, I would not give up the lessons that have come from my failures, even if somehow I could have eluded the associated pain.

Alas, many of us who have had deep introspective experiences may, nevertheless, spend our days and nights perched in the trees and fail to see the forest. As we go about our daily tasks, we draw upon a narrow band of our consciousness to find the knowledge that will help us solve the specific problem at hand. We have learned the most relevant information through experience, and we filter the rest. However, we often go too far.

This filtering causes several gaps in our consciousness. Part II examines them—and also the barriers we erect to awareness. We'll see that filling the gaps in our awareness may open the door to more desirable choices, the way observing a maze from above reveals the way out.

CHAPTER 8

EMOTIONS

Numbness

The scene: *Several fresh-scrubbed young law-firm associates are assembled for a Monday morning staff meeting. All of them are eager to lap at the local fount of wisdom—the senior litigation partner, guru of aspiring trial lawyers—who joins them this day for a primer on trial persuasion.*

The guru waxes: *"I want to tell you today about what I call the 'bi-level' approach to juries. First, you must give them something to 'hang their hat on.' This is your evidence. This is what appeals to their minds. This is what enables them to reach the logical conclusion that you should win. But this is not enough.*

"You must also make them want to find for your client. This you accomplish by appealing to their emotions."

Virtually all beginning trial lawyers get to hear this pragmatic speech in one form or another. The themes of emotional appeals (*pathos*) and logical appeals (*logos*) date back to Aristotle's *Rhetoric*. They are basic to effective argumentation.

For our purposes, the fact that emotions directly determine juror actions is important: it is an acknowledgment that people's actions *are* driven by emotions. But when we ask jurors in the trial postmortem why they decided as they did, they almost never mention any emotional appeals. Why? Because much of the time people function unconsciously. Thus, they are often quite unaware of the connection between their emotions and their actions.

Curiously, although we lawyers will readily accept this proposition concerning jurors—and judges, too, when asked off the record—many of us insist that our own actions are strictly logical. Is it any wonder that we are often clueless about our emotions?

As a young lawyer, I certainly was. And it didn't help my marriage any. Soon after I graduated from law school, my first wife and I went to see a marriage counselor. At some point in the first session he asked me how I felt about something my wife had just said. The conversation, to the best of my memory, went like this:

> **MP:** *"Well, I think her comment has no relevance to the issue at hand."*
> **Dr. Hall:** *"No, sorry to interrupt. Sentences that describe feelings begin with 'I feel' rather than 'I think.'"*
> **MP:** *"Oh, OK. Well, I **feel** that her comment has no relevance to the issue at hand."*
> **Dr. Hall:** *"No, I'm not sure you understand. Words that describe feelings are 'angry,' 'sad,' 'happy,' 'afraid,' 'content,' 'impatient,' and so forth."*
> **MP:** *"Oh, OK. I get the idea. But I don't know how I feel. I don't feel anything."*

Lawyers filter out emotions. Our gut reaction to anything that requires delving into our own emotions is to dismiss it as being "too touchy-feely."

There are several reasons why most of us, not just lawyers, do not fully experience our emotions. One reason is fear. To acknowledge that we're influenced by emotion can be frightening, for it's a concession that our behavior is influenced by something over which we have little control. Since being out of control breeds nervousness, we fight awareness of both the out-of-control feeling and the emotion that bred it.

A second reason is that we often get so involved in what we are doing that we literally don't have time to experience feelings. We simply act and react. Early in my career, I recall being asked to describe a typical day. I began by replying, "The pace is frenetic." If anything, that was an understatement. I would fly from appointment to appointment, catch phone calls on the run, and speed non-stop to depositions and court appearances. In fact, I'd be lucky to be able to read my mail, much less dispose of it, on the same day I received it. I'm sure if we'd had cell phones then, I would have been glued to one. Under such circumstances, it was difficult to notice any feelings. I realized that for the same reasons athletes can play hurt without noticing the pain, those of us who have extremely active lives can conduct them without being conscious of the feelings that our activities trigger.

A third reason is the professional training that many of us get. Law schools, medical schools, engineering schools, and MBA programs, among others, all emphasize analytical problem-solving. In law school, for example, we're taught that emotions have *no* place in legal decision-making. Our job, we're told, is to analyze cases dispassionately. The carryover effect can be enormous. Soon after finishing law school, I took a test to determine my predominate communication style. The test posited four categories:

- Thinker (the analytical approach).
- Feeler (the emotional approach).
- Sensor (the action approach).
- Intuitor (the intuitive approach).

My "thinker" score far outstripped my scores for the other styles. What was habitual with me was the careful, step-by-step analysis drilled into me in law school.

Lastly, we stifle emotions because it often hurts too much to feel them. Throughout our lives many of us will suffer successive painful events. Instead of repeatedly enduring the pain, we numb out. For example, several of my physician friends have commented on how few doctors, themselves included, are in touch with their feelings. They attribute this phenomenon not only to their medical training, but also to the fact that they are in contact with so much pain that they have conditioned themselves to suppress it, even repress it.

Awakening

To become more conscious of our emotions, we must teach ourselves to *take time* to notice them.

Although it may be difficult sometimes to disengage from pressing tasks, an emotion check may actually save time. If, for example, we stop to recognize that anger is driving us to write a nasty letter or to plot and scheme revenge that will ultimately not get us closer to our original goal, we can choose to spend our time more productively. Even though my own life is busier than ever, my noticing my emotions allows me to use the time I have more effectively.

Taking time to meditate or just to think about things can help to acquaint us with our feelings. But merely taking time may not be enough. Sometimes, as I myself learned, viewing ourselves on videotape can help us read veiled feelings appearing on our faces. A few years ago, during a seminar, I participated in an exercise designed to help participants let go of negative emotions such as fear. My face was displayed live on a TV screen via a video camera. I saw a fear in my eyes of which I had been quite unconscious. A little introspection enabled me then to discover the source of the fear.

Since making a conscious effort, I have become more aware of my emotions. During one three-and-a-half-week trial a few years ago in which I was averaging less than five hours' sleep a night, I became so aware of the toll that the pain of combat was taking on me that I cried in my office. And later, when the jury came in for my client, the sheer relief and gratitude that I felt once again brought tears to my eyes.

But if emotions are so painful, and even distracting, why would one even want to allow them to surface? What's the payoff? In his extraordinarily insightful book *Emotional Intelligence, Why It Can Matter More than IQ,* Daniel Goleman provides a compelling answer:

> ...[T]he ability to monitor feelings from moment to moment is crucial to psychological insight and self-understanding. An inability to notice our true feelings leaves us at their mercy. People with greater certainty about their feelings are better pilots of their lives, having a surer sense of how

they really feel about personal decisions from whom to marry to what job to take. (43)

In other words, once we are aware of our emotions, we need no longer be so controlled by them. What are the emotions that control lying and other repugnant behavior? The short answer is fear. In Chapter 1, our chief fears, we saw, were of annihilation and humiliation. In Chapters 2 and 3, we saw those same fears operating in hardball and in getting physical. In Chapter 4, we discussed two fears that underlie death by tedium: loss of control and humiliation. In Chapter 5, we explored how two other common fears—the fear of personal worthlessness and appearing weak—often generate greed. We saw how these fears are common to all human beings, not just lawyers.

Once we are aware of our fears, we have the opportunity to replace them with another, more effective basis for acting. I'll explain how in Part III.

But we can take the next step of more effectively resolving conflict only if we overcome the temptation to deny emotions, like anger, that we believe are negative. For example, I have often been asked if I am angry; almost instinctively, I've replied, "No." Emotions like anger seem socially unacceptable. But if we deny them, we are powerless to keep them from controlling our behavior. So, once we know an emotion is there and that denying it isn't a useful option, we're free to respond effectively rather than reflexively.

CHAPTER 9

RELATIONSHIPS

Most of us have one great difficulty in life, and
that is to see ourselves as others see us and to see
the other person as he sees himself.
— Arthur Miller (Evans 33)

A lawyer acquaintance of mine is notorious for writing
obnoxious letters that often provoke hostility. I once
asked the man, whom I respect as a very intelligent and
effective lawyer, if he would serve on a Continuing Legal
Education program that I was organizing on aggression
and hostility. "Sure," he said. Then I mentioned something about aggressive letters and the effects that they
have. Looking baffled, he confessed, "I didn't realize a letter could be aggressive"!

If we are often strangers to our own emotions, we are
also often clueless as to how our actions affect others. We
saw some examples in Chapters 2 and 3, where lawyers'
overt hostility was quickly reciprocated or, less often, was
met with more effective aggressive action, such as when
Mr. Piersall succeeded in sanctioning and disqualifying the
opposing lawyer, who'd called him a liar. When we're hostile, we imagine that the other side will roll over and give
up, realizing the obvious error of their ways. We're thinking, "They deserve what we're doing to them, and they
know it!" Or we're thinking, "They have no right to be
offended and to respond as if they are, so they won't."
Such a mindset explains the surprise and outrage we feel
when our hostility is reciprocated.

Of course, when we're unconscious of our impact on others, they behave in ways we don't expect and for which we may be unprepared. We lose control of the process and are less effective. Remedying this failing requires that we become conscious of our relationships.

Human relationships are typically in a state of flux, like most everything else in life. We intuitively know, for example, that the kind of relationship we have upon first meeting is apt to be superficial—it's a feeling-out time. Similarly, we've all experienced conflict with other people—and sometimes the gratification of making-up and bonding even more closely. The point is, relationships tend to go through phases.

At any given time, in fact, they're apt to be in one of four major phases. Psychiatrist M. Scott Peck calls them "pseudo-community," "chaos," "emptiness," and "community" (88-103). These phases or states appear to be universal, though they often go by different names. Management consultants sometimes refer to similar group dynamics in work settings as "forming," "storming," "norming," and "performing" (86). Psychologist Yvonne Agazarian, herself a trainer of psychotherapists, refers in her workshops to the four stages as "flight," "fight," "intimacy," and "work."[25] Interestingly, the four phases seem to apply to every kind of relationship—from two individuals to groups of infinite numbers. They may even describe our relationships with ourselves.

Dr. Peck's terminology, I think, is especially useful for our purposes because it's more inclusive, so I'll be using it throughout the rest of this book. Let's now look at each of these phases in turn.

"Pseudo-community," according to Dr. Peck, is typified by "conflict-avoidance" (88). In this phase, we're trying to minimize or ignore individual differences. So, for example, we go out of our way to avoid offending. We practice our best manners. If someone says something offensive, we studiously ignore it. If disagreement surfaces, we quickly

---

[25] Drs. Peck and Agazarian both rely on British psychiatrist Dr. Wilfred Bion's work with groups (Rioch).

change the subject. If someone speaks in sophomoric platitudes, we let them pass unchallenged, or maybe even nod
in accord as if we've just heard some profundity. The price
of pseudo-community, it should now be obvious, is that it
crushes individuality, intimacy, and honesty. And the
longer pseudo-community lasts, the more boring it gets.

When new neighbors move in and start making
acquaintances, the entire block typically goes into pseudo-
community. People make a point of exchanging pleas-
antries. If it's late December, one neighbor may wish the
new arrivals "Merry Christmas!", to which they may simply
respond, "Thank you," without revealing that they aren't
Christians and don't celebrate that day. In fact, they may be
secretly offended that their neighbors would presume that
everyone celebrates Christmas, but they won't say so—at
least not in pseudo-community. In new situations, when
pseudo-community often occurs, people are reluctant to
surface differences for fear they won't be accepted, or might
offend someone. In pseudo-community, our fear of potential conflict outweighs whatever gains we think we might
enjoy from practicing emotional honesty.

After a few weeks, the new residents may start construction on an eight-foot fence. If some old-timers fear the
fence could hurt their view, they may check with the city to
see if their new neighbors have gotten the proper building
permits; and if they discover otherwise, they may huffily
inform the city of the illegality. Meanwhile, though, they'll
still be smiling away and saying, "Good morning!"

At some point, however, pseudo-community may give
way to what Dr. Peck aptly calls "chaos." The triggering
event is usually a statement to the effect that someone
should be—or should be doing—something different than
they are. For example, "If you would only accept God in
your life, you'd be a much happier person," or "I'm sick of
your pontificating! You don't know what you're talking
about." Such comments proceed from a mindset, often
unconscious, that assumes, "If I am to continue being in a
relationship with you, you'll have to change." In chaos,
when individual differences surface, we don't try to hide or
ignore them, as in pseudo-community; instead, Dr. Peck says,

we try to "obliterate them" (91)—we try to make others more like us. Chaos, he observes, is marked by "fighting and struggle. It is not merely noisy, it is uncreative and unconstructive." The struggle gets frustrating and seems to go nowhere. In fact, says Dr. Peck, "[I]t is common for the members of a group in this stage to attack not only each other but also their leader" (92) for allowing such unpleasantness.

Back to our "good neighbors." If the newcomers learn that some smiling old-timers secretly ratted on them to the city officials, chaos is imminent. The fence-builders feel betrayed. They're so upset, in fact, that they're willing to risk the pain of conflict. They confront their neighbors, saying, "Why couldn't you have just *talked* to us about the fence? Why did you have to go sneaking around to the city?"

To which the old-timers may respond, "That fence is illegal and we're not gonna let you build it!"

"Well, we'll see about that!" the newcomers may retort, thoroughly provoked. "The city doesn't know what it's talking about anyway. Bunch of busy-body bureaucrats! We're going to see our lawyer."

From here the controversy can escalate to neighbors mobilizing neighbors as allies in the "Great Fence War," and then on to zoning hearings and court battles. In short, full-blown chaos.

What often happens, though, after a taste of chaos is that people retreat into pseudo-community. For example, after discovering that their proposed fence is too high and deciding that fighting the city over a building permit just isn't worth it, the newcomers may quietly settle for a six-foot fence. But they'll probably continue to harbor feelings of betrayal even though the overt controversy is over. Meanwhile, the old-timers may have written off the newcomers as inconsiderate trouble-makers. But neither side voices these sentiments. Instead, they enter into a period of uneasy co-existence—until that is, someone gets a howling dog or cranks up the stereo!

Although the next stage, "emptiness," would enable these neighbors to resolve future conflicts and perhaps even become good friends, that seldom happens when real-life chaos occurs.

"Emptiness" is the transition to "community." Emptiness occurs when we tire of conflict and consciously choose to take responsibility for our part in it so that we may connect with other people. Unlike pseudo-community and chaos, emptiness is something that most of us experience so infrequently that we find the concept difficult to grasp. It's also difficult because its very name, which seems to carry a negative valence, is an initial put-off. But grasping the concept is worth the effort because it's the most crucial phase of community development—in fact, the key to effective conflict resolution.

The concept of emptiness is this: to be open to others, we cannot be full of ourselves. If a cup is full of water, it cannot receive wine. So we must empty ourselves of barriers to effective communication. Dr. Peck lists five of them.

One barrier is "expectations and preconceptions." (95) Expectations are predictions we make based on past experience. My experience, for example, may tell me to expect an opposing lawyer to make a settlement offer of $15,000 in a case involving a back injury to my client. If she offers $1,500 I may think she is being totally unreasonable and angrily retort, "That's ridiculous. We're going to trial!" On the other hand, if I let go of my expectations, I may be able to learn that the reason her offer is so low is that she has a video of my client water-skiing at a time he claimed to be bed-ridden. Similarly, my history of being angrily chastised by a past lover for being late may cause me to come in spoiling for a fight if I'm late for an engagement with my present lover. The problem with expectations is that they prevent us from effectively dealing with present reality.

The same is true for preconceptions, which are assumptions we make about people and situations. Because they are only assumptions, they may be dead wrong. My assumption was dead wrong, for example, when I once asked the question of a rather heavy woman, "When is your baby due?" It's not too difficult to see how such preconceptions may alienate people from one another.

Another barrier is prejudice, which is a negative preconception about someone. It comes in two forms. One is "the judgments we make about people without any experience of them whatsoever" (95); the other is "the judgments we make about people on the basis of very brief, limited experience." (95) Too often, a bad experience—or just hearing of another's claims about such an experience—with a few lawyers, a few members of a minority group, or a few southern white males may cause us to expect others of their group to behave similarly. Or we learn that someone is an ex-con or a public office-holder and immediately distrust them. When we act on prejudices, our targets naturally resent the negative stereotyping.

A third barrier is when we get attached to some ideology, theology, lifestyle, or approach as "the one and only right way" (96). For example, "The *only* way to properly represent your client is to use every means available to beat your opponent" and "Mediation must be the first step in all cases"—are two common refrains of zealous lawyer-ideologues on opposite ends of the spectrum. Similarly, we've all heard platitudes like "The government that governs best governs least," "Krishna is the only path to peace," and "Rush [Limbaugh] is right." Such dogmas leave no room for differences of opinion, which are inevitable whenever human beings meet. Attachments to ideologies provoke people with different opinions to attack one another head on, like comedian Al Franken and Democratic campaign strategist James Carville attacked the "Rush is right" group in their respective best-sellers, *Rush Limbaugh Is a Big Fat Idiot and Other Observations* and *We're Right and They're Wrong*. Such attacks and counter-attacks prolong the chaos and interfere with finding consensus solutions.

A fourth barrier is the need "to heal, convert, fix or solve" (97). During chaos, we believe we are being constructive by trying to make others more like ourselves. When we call for "family values" or parade our religious beliefs, we're actively hoping to convert others to our own views. During emptiness, if we ever get there, we'll realize that these attempts are self-centered efforts to gain comfort through the elimination of differences (98).

A final barrier is the need to control—to ensure a desired outcome. This barrier, Dr. Peck says, is "at least partially rooted in the fear of failure" (99). We've seen this barrier emerge during the chaos of litigation when we lawyers strive to win at all costs. We do this by trying to overpower others, who predictably resist.

Emptiness, continues Dr. Peck, involves sacrifice. It requires that we put our ego aside and let go of our need to be right or look good. It involves recognizing that the way we have conceptionalized a part of ourselves is erroneous. Such a conception is as alive as an arm or leg. And when we are forced to acknowledge its loss, it may be so painful that we grieve it as we might grieve the loss of a limb. For example, I used to foolishly think that I was the perfect boss. But several of my employees told me that I had a nasty habit of criticizing staffers in a belittling way. Seeing that I was breeding more resentment than effective performance, I decided to let go of my need to control with my righteous frustration and instead sought to *inspire* better performance. The part of myself that believed I was the "perfect boss" was sadly mistaken.

Perhaps because emptiness entails experiences like mine with my employees, Dr. Peck calls it "a kind of death, the kind of death that is necessary for rebirth" (100). For some of us, it may be a "fearsome adventure into the unknown" (100). Rather than thinking of emptiness as a rebirth, many of us will incorrectly think of it as annihilation—of self-concepts that we fear to admit are false.

If the fence warriors each had been able to empty of not only the idea that theirs was the "only right way" but also the desire to achieve a specific outcome, they may have been able to find a mutually satisfactory solution. In emptiness, upon learning that the fence was going up, the old-timers might have said, "We certainly respect your right to build a fence on your property, but have you checked with the city on height limitations? The reason we ask is that we're concerned that an eight-foot fence will block our view. Is there a way that you can build it so that it serves your needs and doesn't block our view?"

The newcomers could have responded to the discovery that their neighbors had gone to the city by saying, "We didn't think to consult with you before planning to build our fence. That was pretty stupid of us, and we apologize. Since the fence adjoins your yard, we can understand why you might be concerned. We would like to work with you to find a solution that somehow meets both our needs."

"Emptiness," then, allows us to effectively deal with present reality.

Emptiness is complete when a group has eliminated its barriers to effective communication, leaving a figurative vacuum that pulls the group together into a deep intimacy —a state of true "community." In community, people "communicate authentically, bridge differences with integrity, welcome and affirm diversity, deal with difficult issues, and relate with love and respect."[26] What we were afraid to say in pseudo-community may now be safely said. Instead of reacting to differences with the frustrating conflict typical of chaos, we patiently explore ways to transcend them.

To reach community, our fence combatants would need to resolve not only their differences over fence design but also their communication issues. To resolve these, either side might have said, "We are sorry to have done anything that may have offended you in connection with the fence issue. Being good neighbors and friends to you is the most important thing to us. If you ever need to talk about any issue like that, we want to be able to talk about it openly and respectfully and find a resolution that we can all feel good about."

Given the bliss of community, the power of emptiness, the phoniness of pseudo-community, and the discomfort of chaos, it's tempting to put evaluative labels on the phases. However, that's unwise because each has its place. Pseudo-community is necessary because it is ordinarily not safe, for example, to be totally open and honest upon a first encounter. Chaos may be necessary if we are to

[26] From the "Mission Statement" for the Foundation for Community Encouragement, an organization founded by Dr. Peck.

bring an unspoken issue to the table or to resist another's irresponsible hostility. While raising an issue or resisting hostility is more productive when it proceeds from emptiness, we're sometimes unable to get to emptiness unless we first go through the chaos. And we may need to experience the frustration of chaos to have an incentive to undergo the sometimes painful feelings of emptiness.

An experience with my father may help illustrate the four phases in a more intimate relationship. In what follows, I have added some details to the explanation I gave him, but I've been faithful to the dynamics of our conversation.

Several years ago, my father, my mother, and I were having lunch. I mentioned to my dad that I wanted to tell him about a workshop that I'd recently attended. I said, "Dr. Peck has developed a process, called 'community building,' that helps a group move through the four phases of human relationship so that they can experience a deep intimacy that we rarely enjoy in real life." I then began to explain the four phases. But I could see his mind was elsewhere. He appeared to listen but he wasn't hearing anything I was saying. At this point, we were in pseudo-community. He was politely "listening" without saying what he was really thinking, while I was obliviously rattling on. When I finally noticed that he was distracted, I said, "Pop, you're thinking about something else, aren't you?"

"Oh yeah, I guess I was," he said. "I was thinking about a deal that we were working on in the office this morning."

"Well, would you like to keep on thinking about that deal, or would you like to hear about these phases of community building?" I asked, genuinely offering a choice.

"Actually, I'm ready to listen if you still want to tell me."

So I continued. "The first phase that I was talking about," I said, "was 'pseudo-community.' You and I experienced it just now when I was talking and you weren't listening. During that phase, we aren't saying what we really feel. We're just being polite and not really communicating openly. We may convey some information, but a whole lot of what is really going on between us isn't being said. It's like in the movie *Annie Hall* when Woody Allen and Diane Keaton are making first-date small talk and the subtitles are describing their actual thoughts, laced with lust and self-doubt.

"The second phase is called 'chaos.' During this phase, we express our need to have other people be different. For example, if, when I noticed that you weren't listening, I'd said, 'Dammit, Pop, every time I have something important to tell you, you never listen!', I would have provoked chaos. The message would have been that I wasn't happy with how you were being and that I wanted you to change. You may have then gotten defensive and said I should understand because your deal is important and that I had no right to feel the way I do. If you'd done that, you then would have been wanting me to be different from how I was.

"But instead of creating chaos, you and I fortunately went into the third phase, called 'emptiness.' Usually, groups—and individuals, for that matter—will go through chaos before they reach emptiness, if in fact they ever do. We were able to skip chaos because I was able to empty of my impulses to create chaos, so I never started a fight, and you were able to let go of your need to be somewhere else. 'Emptiness' is where we look inward and take responsibility for our contribution to the chaos and pseudo-community. In emptiness, we make space within ourselves to receive others. This is a 'letting go' phase. It's where we let go of barriers to communication and to connection with other human beings. We let go of the need to change others. In this case, I let go of my need to have you listen to me. I gave you the space to continue to think about your deal if that's what you needed to be doing at the time. I was also able to distinguish between the facts—that you weren't listening—and a possible negative interpretation of those facts—that 'you don't care about me enough to listen!' Although you could have gotten defensive and hung onto your right to be thinking about whatever you wanted to, you let go of your need to be somewhere else and paid attention. This is a transition phase that enables us to go into the fourth phase.

"That fourth phase is called 'community.' In this phase we've been able to communicate openly. You had the space to say you needed time to process your thoughts about your deal, if you'd had the need. I have now felt you have genuinely heard what I've said and that we are present with each other and are being open. And, because I think that you have really heard me, I feel close to you now." I gave him a smile, and he returned it.

In community, we treat one another with honor and respect. We treat others as we would want to be treated.

Our Relationships with Ourselves

Reflecting on my own personal development and observing that of others, I've discovered that the four phases of human relationship describe not only our relationships with one another, but also our relationships with elements of our own personality.

When we ignore how our actions contradict our professed values, we're in pseudo-community with ourselves. We're not telling ourselves the whole truth about ourselves, or we may be lying to ourselves. Why do we do this? We do it to avoid facing the conflict between our real and idealized selves. So we busily justify our conduct and try to rationalize it, even though we secretly know that we're on shaky ground. On the outside, meanwhile, we will just as busily hide ourselves from others and perhaps lie and mislead them.

Much of our denial consists of denying the very parts of ourselves that may cause us to be unethical. For example, most of us believe that when confronted with a difficult situation, we will act with integrity. When reading in the introduction to this book about the electric-shock experiment in which 62% of the subjects administered up to 450 volts, most of us would imagine ourselves being part of the 38% who refused to be so brutal. But would we? There is a parable about a rabbi who was asked whether he would keep some money he found on the ground or try to return it to the owner (assuming there was some chance of finding the person). He replied, with utter candor, "I don't know, but I hope that I would have the moral strength to return it."

In the workshop role-plays described in Chapter 1, in which over 90% of the lawyers committed flagrant ethical violations, half of them continued to justify their failure even after an expert in ethics explained how it specifically violated the rules of ethics!

In sum, when we deny or justify our perpetration of unethical conduct, as these lawyers did, we are in pseudo-community with ourselves.

Pseudo-community ends and chaos begins when we try to obliterate those parts of ourselves that we don't like. Our self-anger, at such times, reflects a desire to suppress a part of ourselves that makes us uncomfortable. We are fighting with ourselves. But while our anger is really with ourselves, we don't experience it that way. Instead, we externalize it—we project it onto another. For example, one of the things I don't like about myself is my tendency to give unwanted advice. I may direct my anger with that part of myself at anyone else who offers unsolicited counsel. I may react by thinking, "How could you possibly think you have anything worthwhile to tell me?" Another example from my own experience is in the conversation I described at the end of Chapter 2. There I disparaged lawyers who threaten physical violence because I don't like that part of myself that would like to do the same. Another example is the reaction of many people to President Jimmy Carter's famous confession that he occasionally had "lust in [his] heart." Our sharply judgmental reaction reflected our own pain in reconciling lustful urges. This judgment is an additional instance of scapegoating[27]—judging another harshly for having a characteristic that we don't want to acknowledge in ourselves.

All of us, no matter how controlled, have the capacity to fight with ourselves and others when our fear is sufficiently aroused. We may fear humiliation, loss of control, annihilation, powerlessness, or just being wrong. If our self-esteem is based on appearances of wealth, success, power, invincibility, or perfection, we may fear their loss.

[27] In psychology, this phenomenon is called "projection," defined as "an unconscious defense mechanism in which a person attributes to someone else unacknowledged ideas, thoughts, feeling and impulses that he finds undesirable or unacceptable in himself" (Dorland 1362).

Whatever the fear-based vulnerabilities of lawyers, the hostility within the civil-justice system zeroes in on them like a constant barrage of smart bombs. The emotions triggered are so strong that the body literally cannot contain them, with the result that they come exploding forth, inevitably directed at a target. I recall when other lawyers' words have felt like a bludgeon. I have wanted to reach across the table and jerk their tongues out with a pair of vise-grips. I have been angry at the part of myself that I see as weak or wrong, and so I try to overpower my opponent or make him or her out to be wrong. Such feelings notify us that we are in chaos.

When we're in chaos, taking responsibility is what we think someone *else* should be doing. But when we're in emptiness—or what I sometimes call "responsibility"—we look inward and acknowledge the ways that we ourselves have failed to act with integrity; we also acknowledge the parts of ourselves with which we have been angry. We empty of our barriers to accessing all parts of ourselves. In short, we see the truth about ourselves and not only accept and forgive the parts of ourselves that we denied in pseudo-community and fought in chaos, but do so lovingly.

If our acceptance and forgiveness are grudging, we will continue to deny those parts of ourselves when they next surface, as they inevitably will. My inclination to give unwanted advice is a good example. I know that tendency comes from a desire to be affirmed and appreciated for my sagacity. That desire was paramount when a friend was telling me about her work as a leader in a certain organization. Almost before she was finished, I jumped in to suggest several "next steps." Although I immediately sensed her irritation, I defensively thought, "She doesn't know good advice when she hears it." Only later did I realize that all she'd wanted was acknowledgment for her own leadership activities that she had just described to me.

Before the conversation with my friend, I had only grudgingly accepted my own desire to be affirmed and appreciated. As a result, I could not admit to myself that my own needs were driving my behavior rather than the needs of my friend. The grudging part of my acceptance

existed in my psyche like a locked door to a dark base-
ment room where ugly secrets are kept. Had I lovingly
accepted my need for affirmation and appreciation, those
needs would have been more easily seen—in the well-lit
rooms of the main house of my mind. It would have been
easier to say at the time, "I can see that my offer of advice
was more out of my needs than yours. I just want to
acknowledge the accomplishments you've made as a
leader in your organization."

Lawrence Kushner says that whatever we might call a
"higher power" resides even in the evil within us. In
emptiness, we own it and turn the evil into good:

> We go down into ourselves with a flashlight,
> looking for the evil we have intended or done—
> not to excise it as some alien growth, but rather to
> discover the holy spark within it. We begin not by
> rejecting the evil but by acknowledging it as some-
> thing we meant to do. This is the only way we can
> truly raise and redeem it....
>
> We receive whatever evils we have intended
> and done back into ourselves as our own deliberate
> creations. We cherish them as long-banished chil-
> dren finally taken home again. And thereby trans-
> form them and ourselves. When we say the
> ...confession, we don't hit ourselves; we hold our-
> selves. (78-80)

If we do not compassionately accept the unlikable
parts of ourselves, we will continue to defend against
acknowledging their existence by scapegoating others, as I
initially did with my friend who didn't want my advice.
When we reject the parts of ourselves that are angry
tyrants, macho bullies, or weak little boys and girls, we
reject those parts in others. When we lovingly accept and
forgive those parts of ourselves, we can accept them in
others, too.

By accepting our banished children, we redeem ourselves. We can acknowledge our angry machismo and,
instead of trying to hurt someone, we can use the energy

behind it to protect our clients' interests or to hit a solid golf shot. We can accept the weak little child inside who wants to compensate for his weakness by throwing a hostile tantrum, and instead acknowledge the weakness and ask to be comforted by someone we trust.

Surprisingly, emptiness requires that we question even our past successful behaviors when they get in our way. If we are too attached to them, we may fail to draw upon more effective aspects of our personalities in certain circumstances. For example, in many businesses, managers use a directive style. It seems effective, if only because employees know that their continued employment depends on their being compliant. But when these executives use the same management style with volunteers in community-service projects, the volunteers may not respond well to orders because they're volunteers. In order to rediscover an ability to inspire others, the executive must first empty of the attachment to a directorial management style.

The process of emptiness enables us to be in community with ourselves. Our parts are no longer hidden or excluded from our being as they would be in pseudo-community, nor are they fighting with one another as they would be in chaos. Rather, we feel complete and self-aware. Our parts are integrated. We're able to freely and openly communicate with them. We can access them when we need to act, and they won't subconsciously undermine one another.

For individuals, like groups, the process of emptying is cyclical, so the phase of community is hardly static. We continually discover parts of ourselves that we may have been repressing and realize that our apparent community was only pseudo-community. As new vulnerabilities are triggered, our internal community phase goes into chaos until we empty again, and so on.

Motivations During the Phases

In litigation, as with other situations involving an unresolved conflict, each of the four phases is characterized by certain operative questions reflecting our motives at the time. These questions also determine when we lie and engage in other repugnant behavior, including blaming and justifying, as opposed to when we act responsibly.

In pseudo-community, the operative question is, *"What can I get away with and how can I get what I want?"* Pseudo-community, as its name implies, is the phase in which lying often occurs, although pseudo-community can also exist with little or no deception. Pseudo-community may be just a "testing-the-waters" phase—the phase of small talk and sizing one another up—so that we can maneuver to obtain our desires. It is characterized by *apparent* cooperation. This apparent cooperation is clearly operative when lawyers lie in settlement negotiations, or falsely claim that documents don't exist that they would otherwise be "happy" to turn over. We lawyers justify ourselves with convenient rationalizations. In this phase, we may interminably drone on in depositions and smother one another in endless paperwork.

In chaos, meanwhile, the operative question is, *"How can I prevail over my opponents, and what can I do to hurt them?"* Lying may still occur in chaos, but the focus has shifted from apparent cooperation to outright hostility. In chaos, we lose sight of the objectives that began the conflict. The goal now is simply to best our opponent, regardless of whether that advances us toward our original goal. For example, we get physical, play hardball, and use paperwork offensively. Meanwhile, we glibly justify our own questionable conduct and relentlessly blame the opposition.

In emptiness, the operative question is, *"How am I responsible for bringing about or prolonging this conflict?"* We turn inward, viewing our own conduct through the eyes of a fair-minded third party. We discover how something we've said could have offended, or why our own conduct was inconsistent with our system of values or the results we seek. We get in touch with the fear that has driven us in pseudo-community and chaos. We summon the courage to acknowledge that all of this negativity is a part of us. And then *we let it go.* In this stage we adopt the single most powerful antidote to unproductive conflict: *we assume responsibility for our contribution to it.*

In community, the operative question is, *"How can we work together to get our needs met?"* When we are in community with others, we take responsibility for getting not only our own needs met, but also the needs of the group as well, be it a group of two or 2,000. As each of us follows the Golden Rule, to "Do unto others as you would have them do unto you," we afford others the same right to be satisfied with the outcome of the transaction as we afford ourselves. In this stage, we can (1) feel connected, (2) engage in truly productive work, and (3) avoid unproductive conflict.

Competition and the Four Phases

It's useful to understand the relationship between the four phases and the key dynamic of competition so pervasive in the civil-justice system and society at large. As we shall see, the primary reason for recognizing the phase in which it's occurring is that the phase may affect whether we derive satisfaction from the competitive process. Competition may occur in each of the four phases. In pseudo-community, competition is at worst boring and at best only minimally beneficial. In chaos, it's downright painful and frustrating. But in emptiness and community, competition may be richly rewarding.

Either ethical or unethical competition may occur in pseudo-community. If opponents are ethical, they're trying to get away with whatever they can within the rules. If they're unethical, they're trying to get away with whatever they can, period. (Some examples of the latter: golfers not counting short putts they happen to muff, tennis players calling their opponents' close shots "out," lawyers and clients engaging in deception, etc.) If the other side never discovers the deception, the unethical party "gets away" with something. Even when both sides are being ethical, the level of trust is so low in pseudo-community that the other party may suspect they're being had even when they aren't. Although we may politely remain silent about our suspicions, we end the day with a slimy feeling and vow to avoid playing with such an opponent again. If we *know* we've been cheated, our vow will be still more emphatic.

Should we manage to win and thus feel vindicated, we won't be glad we played. And should we lose, we may feel doubly cheated.

Even when we're engaging in "ethical" pseudo-community, as I did when exposing the lies of the wife-beater, the end result in a lawsuit is forced upon the losing side. If the winning side is the plaintiff, the plaintiff gets only what it can obtain by force. Sometimes this may make the plaintiff whole and be satisfactory, yes. More often, however, by the time the plaintiff pays for the costs of doing battle, he or she comes out less than whole. A "winning" defendant will always pay the litigation costs to be vindicated.

If competition occurs in chaos, it is not merely aggressive but overtly hostile. Competition, by its very nature, is aggressive, of course, in the sense that one is seeking to win a contest. But when we enter chaos, we become hostile because our primary objective is to win at another's expense. In sports, so long as the objective is simply exercise, or skill-building, or camaraderie, or even winning a reward, our behavior is competitive/aggressive but not necessarily hostile. Similarly, in litigation, if the objective is to justly settle an honest difference of opinion, our behavior may be competitive/aggressive but not necessarily hostile. But hostility can instantly erupt when, say, someone accuses another of cheating, or when one tennis player hits an overhead into another's midsection, or when one golfer distracts another during a key shot. Then, the objective is not only to win the reward but to make the other side lose, and the contest has become hostile. In Chapters 2 and 3, we saw hostility invariably begin with a perceived provocation and a response in kind, resulting in the desire to make the opponent lose. The result of competition that ends in chaos is highly unsatisfying. Though again we may feel the jubilation of victory if we win, along with self-righteous vindication, we will feel beat up in the process and secretly wonder if the result was worth it. Losing, meanwhile, will feel like death. And, win or lose, the battle will be exorbitantly costly.

During emptiness, our focus shifts from trying to prevail over our opponent to examining whether we ourselves are playing fair or adding to the hostility. In sports, we acknowledge or apologize for angry outbursts, for bending the rules, or for other lapses in fairness. In litigation, we take responsibility for unnecessary provocations and hostile responses. We apologize for erroneously attributing bad motives to our opponent, losing our temper, or even misleading our opposition. We let go of our righteous indignation or rigid attachment to a specific result. We stop posturing and engage in an honest and open discussion about our own strengths and weaknesses. Our disclosure of our shift in attitude will hasten the transition from emptiness into community.

When we make the transition through responsibility into community, competition may produce highly satisfying results. In community, competition becomes a tool that may be used to meet the needs of the competitors. How we play the game is now more important than whether we win or lose. When two good friends engage in a spirited game of tennis or a round of golf to get some exercise, enjoy the outdoors, and hone their skills, win or lose, they'll both be glad they played—even if they had a little bet riding on it, such as "Loser buys the beer." When litigants and lawyers settle an honest difference of opinion fair and square, win or lose, they may be glad they played. The "transaction costs" (expenses of litigation) are minimized because the focus is on meeting the ultimate objectives of the competitors, such as obtaining fair compensation or paying a reasonable settlement, rather than prevailing over the opponent.

A second reason it's important to recognize the phase in which the competition is occurring is that the phase may determine whether we can rationally decide to shift to a cooperative process.

In pseudo-community, because our suspicions are high and the level of trust is low, we fail to see that one alternative for getting our needs met is to shift to a cooperative strategy. We're stuck in our fear that if we play Y, the other side will play X. Because we cannot overcome this hurdle, like my group in the XY game, we continue competing even when cooperative strategies may be more effective in achieving the results we seek.

In chaos, once the hostility begins, it assumes a life of its own, quickly escalating out of control. We start heading down a road chosen out of fear in response to some perceived provocation. Rather than seeking the most direct route to the destination we would choose if only we stopped to reflect, we are pushed by fear down a road with no destination. The litigation selfishly distracts us from whatever thwarted objective started the fight. Now, it is the desire to prevail over our opponent that prevents us from discerning cooperative strategies that may more effectively accomplish our desired results.

We can see, then, that lying and other repugnant behavior are not only affected by the status of our relationships with one another, but also are a *function* of our relationships. It doesn't matter how many rules or creeds we promulgate, whether we are in mediation or litigation, or in or out of tort reform. In all of those contexts, we may still operate in pseudo-community and chaos, and those relationship phases permit lies and deception, hostility, and greed. Thus, *only by changing the status of our relationships can we truly eliminate unproductive conflict.* When we are in genuine community, such conduct is, by definition, unthinkable.

Here, then, is the secret of Randy's miraculous transformation from greedy and deceptive XY Game player to leading advocate for cooperation that we witnessed in Chapter 1. Whereas the participants played the XY game at the beginning of the workshop while in pseudo-community, the final game occurred after the class had built a genuinely intimate community. The power of that connection was irresistible even to the likes of Randy.

What can each of us do to build such community in each of our relationships? The answer lies in . . .

[See below]

CHAPTER 10

INTEGRITY

Gaps in integrity—between our actual beliefs and our professed beliefs, and between our professed beliefs and our actions—are as hard to see as our own eyeballs. To see the inconsistencies requires that we hold up a mirror to ourselves, and even then we fog the mirror with our own breath—the many defenses and rationalizations that cloud our vision of integrity lapses.

Even the most pious sometimes just profess righteousness. I once took a deposition of a ranking clergyman in a large Dallas church. I asked him whether he understood how important it was to tell the truth because he was under oath. He replied, looking me down his nose, "Yes, I do. For that, and many other reasons." He then proceeded to lie straight-faced in an attempt to prevent an injured claimant from recovering from his church's insurance company!

As for my own lying at that time in my career, about the only thing I can say in my defense is that I was not as self-righteous as the hypocritical preacher. I was mostly unconscious of my lying. I realized in retrospect, though, that lies slipped out of my mouth like daily emissions of airborne pollution. The air on which they were borne looked like any other air; it was just there every day. But, like air pollution, lying was toxic. And, for the longest time, I did not even notice my lying enough to see that it was inconsistent with my commitment to being truthful.

Not only may individuals have integrity gaps, but entire professions may, too. For example, the legal profession declares in Rule 8.4 of the ABA Model Rules of

Professional Conduct that "It is professional misconduct for a lawyer to...engage in conduct involving dishonesty, fraud, deceit or misrepresentation" (105). Of course, as we have seen, there is often a substantial gap between this standard and our behavior. I have asked several audiences numbering hundreds of lawyers, "How many think that a lawyer should never lie in the course of representing a client?" Almost all raise their hands. I then ask, "How many of you have never lied in the course of representing a client?" A smattering of hands. I then ask, "How many of the rest of you believe those who say they have never lied in the course of representing a client?" Virtually no hands! Walt Bachman, in *Law v. Life*, suggests that "[t]o a lawyer representing a client, honesty means [merely] the absence of fraud or perjury" (73). In short, you can lie all you want as long as it doesn't meet the definition of a crime.

In addition, there is a gap in what we profess in our houses of religious worship and what we do in everyday life. Texas Tech Law School devoted much of a recent *Law Review* issue to the conflicts that we lawyers face between our spiritual beliefs and the demands of daily law practice. Such gaps are not unique to the legal profession.

Noticing the Ugly Truth

After many years of law practice, I stumbled onto Sisela Bok's best-seller, *Lying*. As I read the examples of lying and the justifications offered, I had the dubious honor of seeing myself in print. I also began to recognize my own justifications—and, more importantly, the cost. I began to feel slimy. I asked myself how I could maintain the appearance of a respectable lawyer who preached ethics while also telling lies, large and small (and usually plausible), on a daily basis.

To begin my return to integrity, I decided to notice my lies.

This conscious self-monitoring made me squirm. I hadn't realized how often I succumbed to the temptation to lie—and for how many reasons. I lied to avoid complicated explanations. I invented excuses. I rationalized. I manipulated. I failed to disclose. I told outright whoppers. I found that I agreed with another lawyer with whom I discussed lying who said "It's just easier" than telling the truth.

Now, I struggle every day with the temptation to lie, just because it *is* often easier than telling the truth. I must force myself to avoid the temptation to exaggerate events because such exaggerations make for a better story. I catch myself in mid-sentence exaggerating a story just to be funny, and I will confess, for example, "Actually, that's not true. I only ate six donuts in one sitting, not twelve." I must be vigilant to avoid slipping back into my lying habit. For me, a lie is like a drink to an alcoholic.

Most people with whom I discuss the phenomenon of deception initially resist acknowledging their own lying, as did I. Most of us have justified our lying so thoroughly that we don't even perceive that we are doing anything wrong. Since we don't, and since lying is wrong, we conclude that we aren't lying. When pushed with an example where we have in fact lied, we respond, "Oh, *that*. Well, that's not really lying because it doesn't hurt anybody." Or we'll offer some other pat justification.

The first step to acting with integrity, therefore, is to notice the places where we fail to do so. This is of course true not only in the area of lying but in the areas of hostility and greed.

Relationship and Process Agreements

Once committed to noticing our lapses in integrity, we'll eventually want to change our actions so as to make them consistent with our beliefs and values. But barriers remain here as well. The barriers are rationalizations and defenses—not just our own but also those of people around us. Since we've built them up over a lifetime, it's hard to maintain our integrity without constant vigilance.

A good way to achieve such vigilance, though, is with the device of relationship and process agreements. A *relationship agreement*, as the name implies, governs the way we will relate to one another. Marriage vows illustrate a relationship contract in a cooperative relationship. Even in competitive relationships, however, we can have relationship contracts, such as agreements to treat one another with civility, for example, or to abide by ethical creeds.

Process agreements, meanwhile, are agreements to follow specific processes. For instance, meetings of various civic or business organizations have agreements such as being on time, speaking respectfully, making decisions by consensus, and the like. As mediators, we get parties to agree not to leave before we declare an impasse, and to have a representative at the mediation with authority to settle the case.

At some time in our lives, most of us have made contracts, though we may not have called them such. A contract, in a legal sense, is simply an agreement that may be legally enforced. If I agree to build you a house for $200,000 according to certain specifications, or to buy your car for $12,000, we have a contract. Relationship and process agreements, in the sense that I'll be using the terms, are not legally enforceable. But they do (1) make explicit the tacit assumptions by which we operate, (2) give us an opportunity to agree to operate according to the same assumptions, and (3) set a standard against which we can measure our conduct.

We'll look more closely at the role of relationship contracts in the legal system later. For now, I want to look at how such agreements may foster integrity.

The Integrity Feedback Loop

Suppose we profess to be ethical and civil. How do we know that we really are? Given what we know about our ability to see faults in others far easier than in ourselves, should we trust ourselves to be our only judges? A better approach is to incorporate our standards into a relationship agreement, such as "We will be ethical and civil with each other while working on this case." Moreover, we may expressly agree to provide one another feedback on whether we have lived up to the standards. Here, for example, is the letter I send to other lawyers at the conclusion of my cases:

Dear_____:

In order to better serve my clients and to help me be more professional, I would appreciate your answering the following four questions. Please be totally frank—I will appreciate your candor. These questions have reference to_____, a matter that we recently concluded.

1. Was I civil?

   1___   Very Uncivil
   2___   Moderately Uncivil
   3___   Slightly Uncivil
   4___   No Opinion
   5___   Slightly Civil
   6___   Moderately Civil
   7___   Very Civil

   Comments:

2. Was I ethical?

   1___   Very Unethical
   2___   Moderately Unethical
   3___   Slightly Unethical
   4___   No Opinion
   5___   Slightly Ethical
   6___   Moderately Ethical
   7___   Very Ethical

   Comments:

3. Were there any ways you observed that I:
   (a) unnecessarily increased the cost of representation?
   Answer: Yes ___ No ___; or
   (b) could have been more efficient?
   Answer: Yes ___ No ___.
   If so, please comment:

4. What other ways might I have done a more effective, more professional job?

After you have completed this form, please return it to me by fax or mail at your earliest convenience. A stamped, self-addressed envelope is enclosed. Thanks very much for your cooperation.

                    Sincerely,
                    Mark L. Perlmutter

I don't send these letters in hopes of someday winning a popularity contest. A goal to be liked by opposing lawyers would be inconsistent with my duty to serve my clients. Instead, I have two objectives. First, I want information that will help me live up to *my own* standards, for I know that even after much internal work, I am now and probably always will be better at finding others' gaps in integrity than my own. My second objective, consistent with my adversity to unproductive conflict, is to heal any wounds that may have been inflicted.

I sometimes wonder what life would be like if each of us sent similar letters at the end of each of our relationships and made appropriate apologies or amends. How many lawsuits would be avoided if the first correspondence were an invitation to voice a grievance and offer to make amends rather than a demand for compensation? How many dollars in fees and months of anguish would be saved if divorcing spouses could begin the process in this way? (I have included feedback letters for lawyers to clients, divorcing spouses, and business relationships in Appendix B.)

Moreover, what if we truly sought to learn continuously by making the information contained in the responses available to those with whom we are about to enter into similar relationships, and asking for their help in monitoring our progress? Businesses already have procedures whereby they learn from acknowledgment of failures. In a process called "Failure Mode Effects Analysis,"[28] experts who have themselves completed a project similar to one that a company is about to do, forewarn of potential failures based on the knowledge of their own failings. If we seek to learn from honestly acknowledging our own engineering failures, why not learn from honestly acknowledging our own human failures? Businesses could volunteer the information about themselves that their prospective joint-venturers, suppliers, or distributors now ferret out in

[28] I learned of this process during a personal conversation with Dr. Larry Browning in March 1997. Dr. Browning teaches at the University of Texas at Austin and intends to discuss Failure Mode Effects Analysis in an upcoming publication of his own.

their "due diligence" research, and ask for help in over-coming their past failures. Although few business people would be willing to risk such self-disclosure initially, Organizational Communication Professor and corporate consultant Larry Browning suggests a solution. The disclosures could be made to a third-party facilitator who would help the parties build their trust to a point that they would be willing to make the disclosures.[29]

In personal relationships, such disclosures should be easier to make. When I have begun romantic relationships, I have done my best to acknowledge destructive actions in past relationships. Although I lost romantic opportunities for other reasons, I never lost one because of disclosures of past failings. And if I had lost one, it would have been for the best.

If we continue to acknowledge our dark sides, and ask for support in our efforts to eradicate the resulting behavior, our integrity should improve from relationship to relationship. For example, just making the decision to send the letter and disclose the contents in future relationships has already made a significant difference in my conduct. What if we were all constantly learning in this way? What if we could be comfortable asking for help in monitoring our integrity? What if we could be comfortable giving such help? What would it feel like to help one another in this way? How much unproductive conflict could we avoid?

How much more rewarding our relationships would become! When a relationship begins with this kind of exchange, the level of trust increases dramatically because such acknowledgment implies a willingness to take responsibility. When I discuss my own failings in past relationships, I experience an immediate sense of being trusted. Similarly, I find that since I have begun discussing the confessions I have made in this book about my lying and other repugnant behavior, such discussions have paradoxically engendered trust of me in other lawyers.

---

[29] This suggestion also came during the conversation referenced in the previous footnote.

The payoffs in starting relationships with such disclosures could be enormous. In business, there might not be a need for the multi-page contracts that are now necessitated by the assumption that if the other side can find a way to screw you, they will. Relationships would be less likely to deteriorate into chaos and more likely to move into emptiness. Whether the relationship is between two *Fortune* 500 companies or two lovers, such a beginning implies an opening for the other side to voice appropriate grievances and a willingness to take proper responsibility for problems. If this continues throughout a relationship, unproductive conflict that results in lawsuits is precluded by definition.

I'd like to offer an example from my own experience to illustrate the three stages of the integrity feedback loop. Attached to the first pleading I file in a case is a proposal for a relationship contract. It reads as follows:

Dear _____ and Counsel:

When this case is over, I hope that all parties and lawyers will be able to say that, "Win, lose or settle, we were well served by the justice system." To that end, I pledge to you that I will do my best to adhere to the Texas Lawyers Creed, and particularly its essence, which is to promote ethical, responsible, and cost-effective representation with civility and integrity.

We will work with you to exchange sufficient information to fairly evaluate the case, to make good-faith efforts to settle, and, if we fail to settle, to afford you a fair opportunity to present the merits of your case. We intend to (1) treat this matter as a problem to be resolved rather than as just a case to be tried, which will save money and time for both sides; and (2) avoid playing "gotcha" and thereby reduce the chances of an arbitrary result based on "a technicality."

If you would like to evidence your support of these principles, you and your client may sign this letter in the space provided. Our intent is not to enter into a binding agreement. This letter is rather an expression by each party of our serious and good-faith desire to cooperatively achieve solutions to problems and resolution of claims and disputes in a manner that will avoid engaging in unproductive conflict.

Sincerely,
Mark L. Perlmutter
&
Client

AGREED:
Attorney or Other Representative
&
Client

I've had three types of responses. Some lawyers, plagued by paranoia, think it's some kind of trap or gimmick and don't sign it. Others, while expressing concern about the legal effect of signing it (there is none because I have no intention of trying to enforce it and it is non-binding by its terms), act in accordance with its terms. Some actually sign it.

In addition, I offer to show the opposing counsel copies of the feedback letters I've gotten from other lawyers, and even offer to let them call other lawyers who've failed to return feedback letters. In this way they are apprised of the truth about how I relate during the case.

During the course of the litigation, I may ask the other lawyer how he thinks we're doing under our relationship contract. If I notice myself getting out of line, I'll try to acknowledge that and apologize. If I think the other lawyer is getting out of line, I may ask if he thinks he's being consistent with our relationship agreement: "Do you think that's consistent with our agreement to not play 'gotcha'"?

When the case is over, I complete the feedback loop via the letter we previously discussed.

The Integrity Feedback Loop

Formation of - - - - ➤ Compare conduct to
relationship　　　　　　relationship
contract and　　　　　　contract standards
disclosure of　　　　　　during relationship
personal standards
and needs for
improvement ◄ - - - - Invite/provide
　　　　　　　　　　　feedback on
　　　　　　　　　　　differences
　　　　　　　　　　　between professed
　　　　　　　　　　　standards and
　　　　　　　　　　　actual conduct

The Power of Integrity

Acting with integrity strengthens our advocacy. The third of Aristotle's classic persuasive appeals from his book *Rhetoric*, the forebear of legal persuasion, is "ethos," an appeal based on respect for the credibility of the speaker. But the power of integrity goes largely untapped. How often do we believe something controversial just because we can trust the person saying it?

More often, we observe political speakers or after-dinner speakers and think to ourselves, "I wonder if he practices what he preaches?" When, as advocates, we see the truth as anything that we can make a case for, when we pontificate, and try to convey infallibility, our audiences, be they friends, lovers, business contacts, or juries, see us as phonies.

On the other hand, when we're scrupulously honest, when we act in accordance with our core beliefs, and when we acknowledge weaknesses in our positions and in ourselves, our authenticity is unmistakable. Our listeners can see and hear the ring of truth.

And when they do, they trust us. When we begin relationships with honest disclosure and with relationship contracts, we build the foundation for resolving conflict in community. Although we may periodically drift into pseudo-community or momentarily burst into chaos, we have a familiar place to which we may return.

CHAPTER 11

ORDER

Snow-country drivers know that "black ice" is the product of sleet or freezing rain adhering transparently to road asphalt. Rubber tires get about as much traction on it as leather shoes on a skating rink.

Climbing a hill coated in black ice can be difficult for a driver used to such conditions and impossible for the novice. In Austin, Texas, black ice occurs rarely. Every time it does, you'll find cars spun out in ditches on either side of hilly roads. What's happened? Drivers began their assent with only enough momentum to get partway up the hill. When they tried to accelerate to avoid stopping in mid-climb, the wheels began spinning and their car slid out of control, either back down the hill or off onto the side of the road.

One evening, while driving my son back to his college dorm after a trip out of town, I found the streets covered in black ice. Because I had driven on the stuff before, I prepared myself for one especially challenging spot that involved a curving downhill road leading to a steep climb immediately beyond. Cautiously descending, I picked up just the right momentum I'd need for the climb. But as I started up the hill, I noticed a driver in my lane up ahead beginning to spin his car out. This unexpected hazard forced me to stop before reaching the summit. I motioned for the other driver to go back down by me to the bottom of the hill. Instead, he went only about halfway down, backed onto a flat side-street, and regrouped. Then, deciding to show the hill who was boss, he came screaming around the corner onto the hill, wheels spinning, in another desperate attempt to clamber to the summit. Of course, he never made it. Fortunately, before he could hurt himself or others, a police officer, who had arrived on the scene just in time to witness this last try, gently advised the fellow to turn back.

This young driver was fighting gravity rather than using it. Had he backed down the hill to the side street, turned around, ascended the gentle slope that I had come down, and used the momentum he could have gained from descending it, as I had, he could have reached the summit of the steep hill.

When we are in unproductive conflict, we, too, are spinning our wheels. We get locked together, furiously revolving in one-up-one-down wrestling matches, escalating the conflict out of control without getting any nearer to our original goal. Meanwhile, we are wasting inordinate amounts of energy. We are fighting natural forces rather than using them.

We intuitively know of natural forces that strongly influence outcomes of conflict but we may not fully understand them. Why do most sports teams, for example, consistently win more often at home than on the road? What does it mean to have "the home-field advantage"? Does it mean merely that the actual playing field is secretly designed to cater to the strengths of the home team? Since the rules of most sports (baseball being a notable exception) prevent tipping the scales in such a manner, there must be some other explanation. Is it that the playing field is more familiar at home and the players feel more secure in familiar surroundings? Does the home-crowd hysteria inspire the athletes to try harder? Does the crowd energy actually augment the strength of the players like the invisible forces that have enabled a parent to lift an auto off a trapped child? Whatever the reasons, forces that exist outside of the playing field itself may be decisive.

These forces are the order in the universe. This universal order includes some forces that scientists understand pretty well, like gravity, electricity, and heat energy, as well as others that are more mysterious. When I say "mysterious forces," I don't mean that they contravene natural law; rather, they are mysterious only in the sense that gravity was mysterious before Sir Isaac Newton came along. We simply do not understand fully how and why they operate. But do they really exist? How can we become more conscious of them and access them? Can we learn to use them rather than fight them?

To answer these questions, we must begin at the beginning . . .

Birth

Floating about in the luscious darkness of the womb, we find our every need met. We have food, shelter, and perfect weather. Our bodily wastes are eliminated automatically. Without our slightest effort, we get whatever we require. We need no thoughts and emotion to drive purposeful action. We don't even need to breathe. Moreover, we have no concept that we are separate from the rest of the universe. As far as we know, we are at one with it.

And then we are unceremoniously extruded from the birth canal and thrust into a cold, glaring world, whereupon our lifeline is cut, and we are drenched, wiped, aspirated, and poked. So begins the process of individuating and becoming self-sufficient.

Yet a part of us must long to return to that state of ultimate bliss when we wanted for nothing. We crave to again be inseparable from the universe around us. Such a profound conditioning may explain our desire to merge with another person in an intimate relationship, out of which the reproductive cycle starts anew.

But is this primitive yearning to merge merely a ruse to ensure the continuation of the species, or is it more? As a parent, I know that my desire to connect with other people did not end with the birth of my children. My deepest programming drives me to continue to reach out to other human beings. When I have intimate conversations with friends and lovers, that yearning is fulfilled. It is also met when I have deeply communicated with large groups, either as a speaker or as member of workshop groups. This book itself is driven in part by the same yearning. And virtually all of my experiences with other people convince me that their yearnings (though often submerged) are mirror images of my own.

Does the yearning for merger stop with our longing for human connection? If it did, then our experience would tell us that those who have deep relationships with human beings would find those relationships sufficient; they would feel no need to pursue a connection with transcendent forces like the Tao or a being like God. Yet there are millions of people who have meaningful human relationships and who still search for connection with the transcendent aspects of the universe: witness the number of followers of the world's religions. If this, too, is a part of our programming, why would we be so wired if there is nothing to which we can connect? Is our programming a cruel trick of nature?

I once thought so. As I was growing up, such a connection was always discussed in the context of organized religion. And much of what was presented as religion was difficult to reconcile with my common sense, not to mention my study of science. The idea that there were supernatural forces that were designated as "God" was ludicrous to me. My skepticism lasted many years. And it didn't even occur to me that there might be a way to reconcile a personal connection to a universal order with the principles of natural law. But as the following story illustrates, I am convinced that a personal connection with the universal order is not only possible, but eminently rational.

Boredom

My story begins inauspiciously in the Jewish faith. Other than for an occasional Bar Mitzvah, my parents, brother, and I attended Jewish religious services as a family only on the two high holy days—Rosh Hashanah and Yom Kippur. We were not alone, as evidenced by the fact that while the synagogue itself was sufficient to accommodate the weekly faithful, it was necessary to rent the city's Music Hall to accommodate all the rest of us—the "twice-a-year" Jews.

My earliest recollection of attending religious services was at about age five. Mom wrapped me in an uncomfortable shirt and tie with a grown-up sport coat that would prompt "cute-little-man" comments. I was then expected to sit still for at least two hours. Being a relatively high percentage of the total time I had lived, two hours seemed an eternity. I have wondered how my 20- and 30-something parents would have liked spending the 12 hours in temple that would have been a similar percentage of their lives. In any event, my abject boredom could only be remedied by constantly cutting up with my brother. Our antics were so disruptive that the rabbi was able to work them into his sermon.

From kindergarten until my confirmation at 15, I attended weekly services as part of "Sunday school." During this period, my experience of religious services did not improve, save for my inventing increasingly sophisticated ways to cope with the boredom. I counted every architectural feature in the temple—light fixtures, pews, support columns, ceiling decorations, even the organ pipes. I played Hangman and Tic-Tac-Toe. I learned to estimate the time it would take for a minute to elapse by glancing at my watch, looking away while I counted off 60 seconds, and looking back to see how close I had come. I did this over and over again to where I could get within no more than a second or two.

I failed to see how attending temple was relevant to my life. Congregants seemed more interested in who was wearing what than in genuine worship. Each week, the same prayers would be recited by rote, the same songs would be sung, and I would leave the temple the same as I'd been when I walked in the door, except that I was a little more bored— a little more irritated, too, that I had wasted the time.

When I was a teenager, I disclosed to my rabbi that I didn't see any relevance in organized religion. Like a wise but somewhat aloof father, he opened up his prayer book, pointed to a prayer that began, "Grant us peace, thy most precious gift, O thou eternal source of peace...," and said, "How much more relevant can you get?" At the time, I thought, "I don't need God or organized religion to tell me *that*! It's so obvious."

During college, there were rare occasions on which my parents would successfully guilt-trip me into attending services on the high holy days. By the time I graduated, guilt and the desire to avoid conflict with my parents were my only tethers to the Jewish religion. But even these motivations were insufficient to prevent my marrying a Methodist preacher's kid after my college graduation. She converted from Methodism to Judaism (via a correspondence course) because religion was important to her and she wanted our kids to be raised in one faith. I didn't even seriously consider converting to Methodism because it was hard enough for me to swallow the idea of God, much less the idea of Jesus. I also felt a strong cultural identity. With our history of persecution, I would have felt like a sellout had I converted.

During law school, we dutifully tried to be Jewish. I did it mostly out of guilt and partly to please my parents. We made several attempts to affiliate with a synagogue. We even joined an adult-education class. Our participation in that class—and that synagogue—ended when several members of the class, not realizing that they were causing offense, began discussing how one could ferret out whether someone who was attempting to attend a worship service on the high holidays was actually Jewish by asking if the person's mother was Jewish. My wife felt excluded and discriminated against. That was the last contact I had with Judaism for many years.

Meantime, I really didn't think about God very much because the concept seemed not only irrelevant to my life, but also self-serving—at least in the way some of my acquaintances used God to justify what they wanted, and rulers used God to justify unjustifiable wars throughout history. For others, God seemed merely a concept they'd invented for their own comfort. Such people, I thought, needed a kind of super-functional parent to offer them the love and support they found lacking in humans. Well, that was fine for them, but human intimacy and compassion were fine for me.

I couldn't disprove that God exists, but everything that I perceived was happening in my universe seemed to make sense without a God concept. After all, there were scientific reasons for nearly everything, it seemed, and for what we did not yet understand about the universe, there was more natural law that simply awaited discovery.

For me, a God concept was unnecessary not only to understand the meaning of life, but also to be a good person. It was enough, surely, that I subscribed wholeheartedly to the Golden Rule. Although I didn't always act in accordance with it, I did believe that it was the most practical way for humans to treat one another. After all, it was Rabbi Hillel himself who, when asked to sum up the Torah (the Old Testament), replied by repeating the version of the Golden Rule in use during his time, saying, "Whatever is hateful unto thee, do it not unto thy fellow. This is the whole Torah. The rest is just explanation" (Pentateuch 563). My personal philosophy consisted of the Torah's version of the Golden Rule, "Love your neighbor as yourselves" (Leviticus 19:18), with my own addendum that answered the "why" for me pragmatically, not theistically: "Love your neighbor as yourselves *and we can all thrive together.*"

But I did still consider myself an ethnic Jew, even if only two rituals of Judaism remained a part of my life through my young adulthood. One was Passover, celebrating the liberation of the Jewish people from Egyptian enslavement. I did not celebrate it because of any religious significance, but because I liked the food and the family togetherness. The other was Hanukkah, a celebration of religious freedom. In the United States, Hanukkah involves giving children gifts on each of eight nights. I celebrated Hanukkah with my children so that they would have a positive association with their Jewish ethnic heritage.

In short, neither God nor organized religion had any place in my life whatsoever. Without these traditional avenues to connecting with universal order, I never thought to inquire about *that* concept in any other way. Instead, I complacently clung to the notion that I myself was, for all practical purposes, the center of my universe.

Friends raised in the Christian tradition used to tell me similar stories. Many, like me, were forced to attend Sunday School and church. They were indoctrinated with religious teachings that strained their credulity. Catholics irreverently referred to Mass as "the magic show." Protestants joked about their religious traditions. ("Why do Baptists never make love standing up? Answer: They might be accused of dancing.") And with our rejection of organized religion, we closed our minds to the possibility of connecting with forces greater than ourselves.

Failure

Then, in my early forties, I began to notice things that I came to see as pieces of a grand puzzle.

This process began when I undertook to use Dr. Peck's Community Building process as part of a program I wanted to initiate to stanch a dropout problem in Austin high schools. I had never worked in the schools before and had no training in education. Yet I walked into an Austin high school, spoke to the principal, was introduced to a cadre of teachers, developed with them a collaborative design for the program—and they bought into my vision. Suddenly, we were off and running. The principal had turned over his school to me, in a sense. When I think back on it and consider what a risk it was for a public-school principal to entrust an outsider—a lawyer, no less—with the school's "at risk" program, I shudder.

And the seeming miracles didn't stop there. The program required that funding for teacher training and for hiring staff be in place at several points before the beginning of the school year in which the program was to start. The school district's Curriculum Coordinator took $20,000 out of her budget to fund the initial teacher training on the very Friday that I would have otherwise had to cancel the program. And the week before I would have otherwise had to cancel the second phase of the training, I received a promise from a state agency for $180,000 in funding.

I was somehow striking responsive chords wherever I turned. It seemed that there were forces much more powerful than I at work.[30] I came to realize this late one fireside evening. As I sat alone in my living room absorbed in the majesty of Beethoven's *Ninth Symphony*, I began to consider how extraordinary he must have been to have created such a masterpiece. And this in turn led me to

[30] A seemingly tangential event also contributed to this notion. While we were working on the program together, one of my mentors was diagnosed with a

consider the wondrousness of the power that had created Beethoven himself.

As my ruminations continued, I began to feel extraordinarily small and insignificant, yet simultaneously at one with the awesome forces of the universe. Overcome with emotion, and with tears welling, I glanced up through a high window and found myself saying silently, "I surrender." As these words came to my lips, I felt a profound connection to a universal order and I acknowledged my relative insignificance.

Although the school program ultimately ran into some insurmountable difficulties with which I will not bore you, for me, the gift that came out of the planning and implementation of the project was that for the first time I felt a connection to a universal order and the beginning of my awareness of mysterious forces that transcend all of humanity. Yet the ultimate failure of the program was a double setback, because it also caused me to begin to doubt the existence of such forces. In retrospect, I realize there was a part of me that still saw any forces greater than myself as an extension of my own desires; for, as altruistic as the school initiative had been, its success was my desire—a desire that may or may not have been in sync with transcendent forces.

Return—Teshuvah

During the next several years, my understanding gradually matured. One significant event was a ski trip I took with a friend who had returned to Judaism many years following a Jewish childhood similar to mine. As we drove over a high mountain pass and took in the majesty of the Colorado Rockies, he told me of that return of his.

Newly intrigued, I began meeting with a local rabbi to discuss spiritual issues and get recommendations for books

brain tumor that the doctors had told him was likely to be malignant. A very spiritual man, he called upon many friends who were non-traditional healers to perform rituals and say prayers for him. And astonishingly, when the neuro-surgeon went in to remove the tumor, the mass that had shown up on the brain scans had disappeared. The doctors could never explain it. There had been no "mix-up in the lab"—only a seemingly inexplicable miracle. Since there was no known scientific explanation, I wondered, "What had accounted for it?"

I might read. Slowly, I became convinced that Judaism might have some answers for the question that was burning in my mind: *What is the nature of the universal order?* I then enrolled in a basic Judaism course, where I learned that Judaism subsumes many concepts of God, not just one. The concept that most appealed to me, at least as I understood it, was the one equating God with those processes within natural law that make for the highest fulfillment of people as human beings (Kaplan 102, 103). This concept, which appealed to my rational, legally trained mind, is similar to the ancient Asian Taoist philosophy. Grossly oversimplified, Taoism holds that our task is to stay in, or align with, the Tao—the flowing course of nature and the universe (Watts 37-55). An example of aligning with the flowing course of the universe is climbing an icy hill without spinning our wheels.

I even decided after considerable hesitation to attend a Friday night worship service. Consciously dressing down for the occasion—I wore merely a comfortable cotton shirt (with no tie!), slacks, and sport coat—I entered the sanctuary and took a seat alone. I felt a little anxious because the surroundings were new to me. But, unlike in my childhood experience, I sat quietly throughout the service— and I was anything but bored. The sanctuary felt truly that: a sanctuary not only in space but, because this was Shabbat (the sabbath), a sanctuary in time.[31] It was a time for reflection—to be in the moment, conscious only of my current existence.

And that current existence, I had to acknowledge, was plagued with unrest. I was particularly weary of the daily conflict and hostility I had to endure as a lawyer. Battle-scarred and shell-shocked, I was secretly wanting to do anything but practice law.

While I was thinking these thoughts, we came to a prayer in the service that I found both familiar and entirely new:

---

[31] My first acquaintance with the concept of a "sanctuary in time" was my reading of Abraham Joshua Heschel's *The Sabbath* (3-10).

Grant us peace, Your most precious gift, O
Eternal Source of peace, and give us the will
to proclaim its message to all the peoples of
the earth....

This message of peace seemed directed squarely at me,
to comfort my soul. I felt not only a kinship with the millions of Jews whom I imagined had recited this prayer for
millennia, but also a profound connection with the universe itself. I quietly wept as I realized that the universe
somehow was holding me. The entire experience was like
coming home after a long journey. In Hebrew, this is
called "teshuvah," or return.[32]

But with my teshuvah I also found a new vista like a
resplendent valley unfolding before a climber who's stumbled upon a scenic overlook. I was entering the spiritual
realm. I had a new vision of the world around me that
seemed richer and more meaningful. Unfortunately,
though, the glimpse was obscured by the fogging of my
glasses. If I was to survey the grandeur before me, I would
need to clear my vision.

The clearing I needed was like that required of a young
warrior I'd heard about whose Shogun sent him out to
resolve border encroachments by raiding armies.[33] Though
he achieved success in battle after battle, vanquishing the
invaders with dispatch, the border clashes continued
because he continually failed to identify—and deal with—
the causes of the squabbles. Finally, the warlord sent the
young warrior to see a Zen Master. This sage one handed
him a full cup of hot tea, then proceeded to add even more
until the tea overflowed, spilling on the young fighter. The
youth instinctively reached for his sword. He then collected
his wits and exclaimed, "You handed me a cup of scalding
hot tea and then added more so as to spill it on my fine
clothes! Why did you do that?"

---

[32] The irony that the words of the prayer in this context now meant so
much to me when they formerly seemed so self-evident as to make religion
irrelevant, did not dawn on me until later.

[33] This story is from Stu Penny of Gunpai Corporation.

The Master responded, "You have come here with your mind filled to the brim like that cup of tea. And so it is with all of us. Our minds must be ready to receive. Before we can understand and build, we must have an empty cup."

Interestingly, there's that word "empty" again. Like the young warrior, once we have emptied our "cups," we are open to see reality as it is and receive the wisdom of the universe.

Finding Your Center—Emptying, Part 2

This emptying takes place in two ways.

One way is in the moment. When we let go of the urge to strike a child who provokes our anger, we are emptying in the moment. Similarly, when we restrain the impulse to pass a car on a curve because we are in a hurry, we are emptying in the moment. Responding effectively in the heat of battle or conflict demands that capability.

Martial artists call it "centering." Peter Ralston, the first non-Asian to win the World Championship Full-Contact Martial Arts Tournament in the Republic of China, describes the concept:

> Centering is perhaps the best way to calm our intellect and emotions. Putting attention and feeling in the center region of the body allows a shift in state of being to one that is calm, non-thinking, balanced, aware, in-the-body, grounded, present, and alive. It also coordinates and harmonizes all movement in the body. All actions and movements are done with more power and control when directed by and coming from the center. (9)

The second form of emptying occurs over time and gives us the ability to more easily return to our center. This long-term emptying is like muscle building—the stronger our bodies become, the more quickly and powerfully we can respond in the moment. It is a continuous life process that nourishes our minds and spirits, just as food and exercise nourish our bodies.

Long-term emptying involves becoming aware of past events that may still control our current reactions. For example, a parent may overreact to his child's forgetting her coat at school by inflicting deep bruises with a wooden paddle. As an adult, the woman may explode in anger at a spouse who casually asks, "Honey, did you forget and leave your overcoat at the restaurant last night?" If the adult woman has not emptied of her anger at her parent, the intensity of those feelings may keep her so off balance that she may be unable to center to prevent blasting her spouse. The wounds of childhood have left her vulnerable to reminiscent situations.

With that overview in mind, let's now take a deeper look at how to empty in the moment and center. Later, we'll examine the key vulnerabilities of which we must empty in the long term to increase our ability to center in the moment.

To be open to the forces of the universe, we obviously cannot be filled with our own emotions and thoughts. Fundamentally, we must be open to experiencing the next instant. Instead of thinking about the past or future, we must be, as the saying goes, "in the moment."

How can one experience the feeling of being centered for the first time?

The following series of guided meditations can get you centered.[34] These should be done in order, especially if one has never felt centered before. I suggest that you ask a trusted friend to help you, and that you do the exercises in a quiet, dimly lit place. Begin by sitting comfortably in a chair. Have your partner slowly and soothingly recite these phrases, and follow his or her instructions. Do not answer any questions out loud. Have your partner allow enough time between each phrase for you to complete your thoughts.

1. Relaxation

Close your eyes and relax your breathing. Notice the feeling in your feet. Any tension or tightness there? Any dense feelings? If so, relax the tension. Let your feet just rest. Don't fight the tension or density; just let it be. Accept it as it is. Relax with it. Let it flow. Feel it as it begins to

---

[34] If you have difficulty getting centered, it may help to explore any of your own barriers to being in touch with your feelings.

loosen and work its way through to the skin and dissipate through the pores, evaporating like water turning to steam.

Repeat this litany for the calves, thighs, pelvis, lower back and stomach, upper back and chest, neck, and head.

If you have difficulty staying awake for all of the steps, try skipping the areas of the body that do not contain any tension. Or sit erect with your weight forward and your feet planted firmly on the ground so that you could stand without leaning any farther forward.

2. Visualization—Success

Think about a time when you felt totally successful. (Your partner should determine if you have been able to come up with one by asking, "If you are able to do so, please nod 'yes'.") What are you doing? Where are you? What do your surroundings look like? What are you wearing? Who is there with you? How have you prepared for this moment? What have you overcome to get here? How do you feel? What is the feeling in your arms and legs? Within your chest? What are people saying? If you could see yourselves, how would you look?

Notice how you feel now. What does it feel like to be totally successful, to reach this pinnacle? Are you in touch with your strength? Your power? Clasp your hands together tightly and place them on your stomach, just below your navel. Whenever you want this feeling to return, all you have to do is to clasp your hands together tightly and place them in this same place. Now slowly relax your hands, remove them from your midsection, and return them to a comfortable place. You may open your eyes.

3. Visualization—Love

Think about a time when you felt totally loved. (Your partner should again ask, "If you are able to do so, please nod 'yes'." If you have trouble remembering such a time, your partner should ask you to remember or imagine what it felt like to be in the womb, before birth.) Who is with you? Where are you? What are you doing? What do you see? What are the colors of your surroundings? What is being said? What do you hear? How are you breathing?

What sensations do you feel? How do you feel inside? What does it feel like to be totally loved? Revel in that feeling.

Notice how you feel now. Clasp your hands together tightly and place them on your stomach, just below your navel. Whenever you want this feeling to return, along with the feeling of being totally successful, all you have to do is to clasp your hands together tightly and place them in this same place. Now slowly relax your hands, remove them from your midsection, and return them to a comfortable place. You may open your eyes.

4. Centering your energy

Notice the areas of your body where you feel activity, or where there seems to be energy. (This may be a difficult concept to grasp at first. You may experience energy in your head if your mind is racing in response to a verbal attack, or if you have a stress headache coming on. Your chest may carry feelings related to love and connection with other people. Your pelvic area may carry sexual or other energy related to pleasure.) Do you feel any energy in your legs? In your pelvic area? In your chest? In your head or neck? Let it flow like a river to a site deep within the center of your body about an inch below your navel. Feel it as it travels there. When it arrives, feel it as it swirls round and round into an ever-tightening vortex. As it gradually gets smaller and more dense, feel its intensity, its power—and its peace.

You should be able to re-center by clasping your hands together tightly and placing them on your midsection and then allowing the energy in your body to flow there and concentrate in a tiny, dense sphere. With practice, you may be able to center just by choosing to do so.

Creating this feeling with meditation is valuable because we need to know what it feels like—not only to return to it, but also to know when we are not there.

While centering may seem effortless while we sit comfortably in our armchairs, how can we center in the midst of conflict, when provocations, like head-popping left jabs, jostle us from our center and keep us off balance? When perceived threats raise our fears, we may be nudged or even jolted from our center. Our center of gravity rises and we are easily shaken. Our mind begins racing and our emotions are high with the urge to fight or flee. We hear an unstoppable chatter in our heads. There may be so much energy in our body, or so much density or tension, that we can't meditate it away. We may need time to process—to determine what has triggered our fears and why we can't let go of them. This is what happens when our buttons are pushed, when our vulnerabilities are triggered.

There are two ways to deal with these intense emotions. One is called "bracketed emptying."[35] This means that we put a "bracket" around the need to process—to determine what has triggered our fears. We simply notice them and let them go—for the time being—until we have time for cool reflection and introspection. We may then return to our center.

The second way is to lessen the potential for those intense emotions to occur in the first place by reducing the vulnerabilities that trigger them.

When we face the weaknesses that surface in conflict, we find the most important to be the fear of losing. We are conditioned from childhood to play to win, whether in schoolyard games, grades in school, or athletic competitions. In the hyperbolic words of former Green Bay Packer coach Vince Lombardi, "Winning isn't everything, it's the only thing." And when winning is the only thing, it follows that when we lose, we have nothing. No wonder we fear losing.

Martial artist Ralston agrees that fear is the key distraction that must be overcome to avoid injury:

> ...I noticed that if I wasn't afraid of getting hit, or of winning or losing, that it was easy. I wouldn't get hit! That was the first time I was able to never get hit, 100%...I just saw a fist coming and I'd move. And I saw it all the time because I wasn't stuck on any one. I wasn't worried about it. When I get worried about it, I become afraid of losing. Then I get stuck somewhere and get hit. (ix)

[35] This term was coined by The Foundation for Community Encouragement.

Emptying of fear is no easy answer. As we saw in Chapter 8, it is hard enough to be conscious of our fear. We humans resist acknowledging the negative parts of ourselves. Alexander Solzhenitsyn eloquently observed: "The line dividing good and evil cuts through the heart of every human being. And who is willing to destroy a part of his own heart?" (1: 168). Just as we resist acknowledging the evil parts of ourselves, we resist confronting our fears. But assuming we muster the courage to do so, how can we overcome that fear?

First, we must recognize that fear doesn't exist in a vacuum. Fear always includes a worrisome *consequence*. For litigants, some of the most typical consequences are the loss of money, the loss of freedom, and humiliation. For lawyers, the feared consequences may be malpractice suits, embarrassment, loss of income, loss of reputation, or a sense of failure over losing the lawsuit. Lawyers and non-lawyers alike, in their work lives, may fear loss of money, employment, and opportunities, not to mention the loss of the intangibles that these tangibles represent— self-esteem, power, and security. For lovers, what's at stake may be the loss of attention, sex, understanding, validation, and even the relationship itself. The desire to avoid fearful consequences is a normal part of life.

Yet, ironically, acting on our fears of such consequences increases the likelihood that they'll occur. I recall my first jury trial against a "name" lawyer. I so feared being humiliated that, just before final argument was scheduled to begin, I experienced an anxiety reaction that I confused with a heart attack—at age 27! Needless to say, being focused on my own humiliation kept me from attending effectively to the business at hand. The same phenomenon often operates in sports. We've heard of athletes—and even entire teams—choking when a lot is riding on the outcome.

For me, learning detachment from results proved easier said than done. I first thought that such detachment meant only that I shouldn't fear losing. But then I realized that if I enjoyed winning too much, naturally I would be attached to winning, which was no different from fearing losing.

I found a solution to this conundrum in *The Seven Habits of Highly Effective People*. Here, Stephen Covey counsels us to center on principles in order to detach from results. Although we cannot control results, we have total control over whether we live by the principles to which we aspire (122-128).

For me, this meant that regardless of what I was then engaged in—be it the handling of a legal matter, my relationships with my children and lovers, or any other aspect of my everyday life—how I was *being* was *all* that was important. To invoke a sports metaphor again, I realized that how I play the game is all there is. Winning and losing take care of themselves.

Of course, I still want to win, and I enjoy winning. Just so, I would rather not lose and sometimes experience disappointment at losing. But my sense of self isn't tied up in winning or losing. And whatever the result, I can well tolerate it.

Let me tell you about a recent case I had. The case came to me when an inexperienced lawyer approached me shortly before trial asking for help. Her client, a 79-year-old widower, had fallen over a stocking cart in a big grocery store. It was clear that the plaintiff was not going to get a fair shot at justice with this very well-meaning but hopelessly outgunned novice lawyer. In part because I wanted to see the client get fairly treated, and because my own cases were settling and I was not getting into the courtroom often enough to suit me, I agreed to try the case.

From the outset, though, I was unclear as to whether the cart had been moved in behind my client when he was looking in a milk cooler for a carton of milk or whether he just didn't notice it when he walked by it. If the stocker had "snuck up" behind him, there seemed a good chance that the jury would hold the grocery store liable. But if our client had just not been attentive, I thought it would be difficult for a jury to find the grocery store negligent. Clarification of the issue came during the trial when the defense brought the cart to court. My first awareness of its presence was when I heard it clanking down the hall outside the courtroom! Once it was inside, I even tried very consciously to move it noiselessly so I could argue in final summation that the stocker had carelessly moved it behind my client without warning him. Well, as I ever-so-gently tried to move it, I couldn't stop it from clanking—the damned cart was so noisy that the grocery store should have been cited for noise pollution. There was no way anyone could have snuck it up behind my client.

Even though the jury found for the grocery store, I felt good about my part in the process. With the time I had, I had diligently prepared and aggressively tried the case. I carefully listened to my client and presented his side of the story. Although I pulled no punches, I treated the judge (with whom I had respectful disagreements), opposing counsel, and witnesses with civility. My client, though disappointed with the verdict and with the jurors' reactions to his plight, felt that his side of the story had been forcefully presented.

Just as I experience losses differently than I used to, I experience accomplishments differently as well. Emma Wheeler, the young woman whose tender secrets were broadcast and trampled upon during the mediation described in Chapter 6, brought me a small gift upon the conclusion of her case. It was a matchbox lined with burgundy velvet. In it, there was a tiny figure of a knight in shining armor and a slip of paper that said, "'Consciousness is the only true aristocracy'—D.H. Lawrence."

At one time this gift would have been like a bellows for my puffed-up ego, not only because of Emma's recognition of the job I had done, but also because of her recognition of my level of consciousness. However, when Emma gave it to me I experienced a peaceful, quiet satisfaction.

I experienced a similar satisfaction from both of these recent events because of my detachment from results. I have learned that if I want to be satisfied with the results I seek, I must seek results I can control. For me, it is not whether I win or lose, but whether I conduct myself with integrity.

Seeking to conduct myself with integrity has been an antidote not only to my fear of losing but also to my other fears—of humiliation, of being imperfect, and of lacking money, to name a few. I'm now less likely to have my buttons punched and be knocked off center. And when I lose my center, I can more easily return there by remembering what's really important to me: *Am I acting in accordance with my principles?*

To summarize, when we are centered, we have let go of any attachment to external results and the ensuing fear. We are calm and in the moment. We have broken the filter of fear that colors our perception of reality. In doing so, we have taken our own prejudices and expectations out of the picture. We can see what is. Once we have emptied of our fears and attachments, we can tune into the grand scheme of things like a tiny atomic particle exquisitely resonating with the unified field. We can access the universal order and its enormous power.

The Context Step

After honestly acknowledging our conduct, the next step to preventing or resolving unproductive conflict is to become aware of the context of that conduct. The context involves at least these four considerations that we have explored in Part II:

- The nature of our emotions that trigger it.
- An awareness of how the status of our relationships with ourselves and others relates to our satisfaction with the ultimate outcome.
- An awareness of how our conduct measures up to our personal value system.
- An awareness of the order of things.

If we know our internal status—that we are experiencing the lack of integrity and the fears that may be characteristic of both pseudo-community and chaos—we can choose to empty ourselves of them. Making such an internal shift will not only enable us to be in community with ourselves, but will enable us to powerfully move the relationship itself toward community.

Once we are aware of the universal order, we shall see in Part III how we can access its power to harmonize with and influence events.

PART III

COURAGE

INTRODUCTION
TO PART III

Courage vs. Fear

As we saw in Part I, the lying and other repugnant behavior so pervasive both within and outside the civil-justice system stem chiefly from fear. So too, in fact, does all conduct whose primary purpose is to overpower another. When the object of litigation is to "teach them a lesson," we fear looking weak. When we scream at our children to force them to behave, or scream at our co-workers to bully them into doing things our way, we fear losing control. When we fight with our spouse or partner, we fear being dominated or not getting our needs met. When we bash members of another group, we fear they may do us harm. Marianne Williamson, in *A Return to Love*, declares this simple but profound truth:

All negativity derives from fear.
When someone is angry, they are afraid.
When someone is rude, they are afraid.
When someone is manipulative, they are afraid.
When someone is cruel, they are afraid.
(Williamson 100)

But if fear is behind destructive behavior in conflict, what is the opposite of fear in conflict?

The answer is courage.[36] Courage is both the opposite of fear in conflict and the ability to overcome fear.

Fear causes us to increase the distance between us, whereas courage promotes connecting with one another—

---

[36] I acknowledge that I speak of courage in conflict in a more restrictive way than we commonly think of courage—a willingness to undergo any personal sacrifice to accomplish something good or a willingness to risk death or injury for a cause.

moving closer to one another regardless of the state of our relationships. In conflict, courage enables us to engage our opponents rather than flee. Not only in actual warfare, but in all human relationships, the decision to fight an aggressor rather than flee may bring the combatants closer together. When we flee, we try to remove others from our lives; this, of course, leaves no chance to resolve the conflict. When we fight out of fear, we see the opponent only as a threat to our own wants—this too may drive us further apart. But when we fight with courage, we see more than just a threat: we also see the humanity of our opponent at the same time that we fight to protect ourselves or others or to stand up for our principles. With such a mindset, we move physically and emotionally closer to one another. We in effect say, "You are important enough to me that I am willing to assume the risks of doing battle with you."

For example, when one spouse who has been emotionally injured by the other has the courage to confront the other with love rather than harboring an unspoken grudge or giving up in disgust, he or she seeks closeness in the relationship. Or take this example: Even when England began impressing American seamen, literally kidnapping them on the high seas, our forefathers' decision to fight her in the War of 1812, rather than to appease her, was a decision to move closer in the relationship. And we did so with courage—out of a desire to protect our own freedom—rather than with a lust to destroy the English. Engaging in battle moved us closer than if we had removed our ships from the seas to protect our sailors or otherwise fled. Eschewing conquest once we had the upper hand in battle opened the door to the warm relationship with England that we have today.

Once conflict starts, courage enables us to move still closer by taking the risks of making peace. Acting from fear escalates conflict or causes us to flee; courage drives us toward peace and connection with one another. Courage enables us to resist the temptation to respond in kind to someone who engages in the deception of pseudo-community or the hostility of chaos. Courage moves us from pseudo-community and chaos through emptiness into community; fear drives us the other way.

Courage is not so much an emotion as it is the product of a conscious choice, a way of being. Although the word "courage" comes from the Old French for "heart," I believe that courage depends on our ability to draw energy from the heart and collapse it into the region of the abdomen where we are centered. My own experience of operating from this place is that I feel powerful, safe, invulnerable— at peace, loving. It is the former feelings that permit the latter; when we feel secure we are free to love.

As explained in Chapter 11, centering is emptying in the moment. When we let go of our need to control, to get even, to win, or to dominate, we are emptying and centering. When we replace our fear of losing with a return to the core principles that we choose to govern our way of being, we are emptying and centering. When we find a place that fits into and resonates with the great forces of the universe, like a piece of a hologram, we are centered and empty. It is from this place that we can harness the enormous power of courage.

In short, *courage, in the context of conflict, is the internal state of being, arrived at through emptying and centering, that enables us, with integrity, to take action to bring people, including ourselves, closer to one another.* When we approach conflict in this way, we are engaging in what I call "centered conflict resolution."™

Using The Power

A few years ago, while enjoying a talent show that culminated a weekend retreat, I watched as a gentle man began singing from the heart. Shortly after he began, a young woman sitting next to me spontaneously arose from her seat and proceeded up onto the stage, where she began dancing. With the grace of an angel, her willowy body expressed the lyrics of the song as if she already knew them. She swayed and pitched, flowing in perfect harmony with the moods of the verses. As the singer called up a painful image of loneliness and lost love, the anguish of the entire consciousness of humankind seemed to emerge from the young woman's face. The song ended with a prayer for love and compassion, and her expression radiated the hope of an innocent child as she gazed up beyond her outstretched hand.

Although the audience had clapped for every act up until then, it sat in stunned silence as the song ended. Mirroring our deepest yearnings for love and human connection, this serendipitous duo had so deeply touched the audience that no one could speak.

Later, I introduced myself to the young woman and expressed my admiration for her extraordinary talents. She responded simply, "It wasn't me." I made some flattering protestations and she said again, "But it wasn't me."

For much of that night and for several weeks later, I mulled over her words, "It wasn't me." Well, I thought, if it wasn't her, then who was it? What did she mean, it was not her? Did she mean that it was merely a projection of mine? That I saw in her nothing more than what was in my own heart? And was there more meaning?

Several months later, I gave a speech to over a hundred attorneys in which I explored the themes of courage and human connection among lawyers. It went well. Several people came up to me afterward and said it was the best Continuing Legal Education speech they had ever heard. I was feeling full of myself until I realized that what had made that speech touch the audience was the same thing that had enabled the young woman to touch me: the extent to which she was able to move the audience was only a function of the extent to which she was able to synchronize with the human yearning for love and connection and channel those forces through herself. And so it was with me. The power I attributed to my own prowess as a speaker in fact came from beyond myself, and my *self* was a mere speck by comparison.

This driving force toward love and human connection is the most powerful of universal forces. In fact, it is what gave Senator Lamar (of whom we spoke in the introduction) the power to heal the wounds of North and South. We saw how, according to John F. Kennedy, Senator Lucius Lamar powerfully inspired forgiveness by the North in his eulogy to Senator Charles Sumner. The power of his speech lay in his ability to access the forces of peace, connection, and wholeness. He was able to access the pervasive but previously untapped, unarticulated sentiment for North-South healing and renewal. What's more, it was always there! As he said to his countrymen, "[K]now one another, and you will love one another." His emptiness enabled him to perceive this yearning and tap into it when scores of other less conscious leaders missed their opportunity to shine in history.

When we are in harmony with the peaceful flow of the universe, we are more powerful than when we simply resist force with force. Aikido instructor Tom Crum describes a well-known exercise in which one person extends her arm straight out in front of her, palm up, and asks a friend of equal or greater strength to bend it at the elbow by pushing down on the biceps and pushing up on the back of the wrist. Initially, the trainee will tense her muscles and fight the muscular force that is trying to bend her arm. After a few seconds, her arm will tire and succumb to the superior force. Then she is told to imagine that her arm is a firehose and that an enormous river of water is flowing through it from the center of her body. She even wiggles her fingers to ensure that she is not inadvertently tightening her muscles. This time, the opponent's efforts to bend her arm fail.

Crum explains the phenomenon:

> Just as a fully turned-on fire hose is pliable, yet unbendable and unbreakable, your arm will stay soft to the touch, giving a little but not breaking down because of the external pressure. Your arm is now connected to your own center and to the world through flowing energy. To bend it, your partner has to contend not with a few muscle fibers, but with an unlimited river of energy. (89-90)

As human beings, we are but one form of energy in a unified field of energy. The field is invisible but quite real. Gravity, electrical energy, and magnetic energy all create fields within the unified field. Instead of seeing the world as a collection of independently operating things, quantum physicists tell us that the universe more resembles an ocean of energy (Wheatley 46-57). If two fish are swimming along and one drifts into a tide pool while the other stays in the main current, both may be exerting the same effort but the one in the current will travel farther. In the same way, every conflict exists in the energy fields of the universe. And we can flow with the energy of love and human connection and move ahead toward peace—or we can get stuck.

Just as the river of energy flowing through an outstretched arm is a source of enormous power of the body, our alignment with the forces of connection is the source of enormous power of the mind and spirit.

On the other hand, when we drive one another apart, we are resisting the forces of the universe—spinning our wheels. Illustrative of this phenomenon is a parlor toy consisting of several steel balls in a line, each suspended by thin wire from a support bar so that they can swing freely. When someone lifts an outside ball upward and outward and lets it go so as to strike the end of the line of balls, the last ball on the opposite end will fly out with almost the same force that was exerted by the original ball. This second ball will then return to the pack with a force that will knock the original ball out again. Each time an impact occurs, the ball on the opposite end of the row will fly out slightly less than it did the previous time because the force of gravity resists the outward and upward motion of the balls. If two balls are lifted up and used to strike the pack from one end, then two balls will respond from the other end. This back-and-forth impacting continues until gravity finally saps the balls of their energy, or until the balls on one end are held in place—which will stop the balls on the other end from moving further.

While the balls are hanging undisturbed, they are in equilibrium. But when one of them is lifted so as to strike the pack, it throws things out of balance and "provokes" a responsive blow. We have seen this pattern in the provocation/response syndrome of the civil-justice system. The same dynamic of conflict was recognized by an ancient Chinese philosopher, Lao Tzu:

> For every force there is a counterforce.
> Violence, even well intentioned,
> always rebounds upon oneself.
> (Mitchell 30)

Recent history is full of examples of violence rebounding on itself. The Allies organized to bring down Hitler in World War II, just as the Allies organized to thwart Saddam Hussein's adventures in Kuwait. In Texas, there is a law firm notorious for its hostile tactics. But in recent years it has been castigated by the majority of the state's other lawyers, and its clients have suffered at the hands of judges who expect the worst from this firm. My sometimes overly aggressive brethren in the plaintiff's bar, who have extracted excessive, high-profile verdicts, live ostentatiously, and blow their own horns, have brought animosity on themselves from the public, state and federal legislators, and judges who resent self-importance. Similarly, the zeal with which House Democrats pursued Republican Speaker of the House Newt Gingrich, seeking to use his ethical troubles to defeat his bid to be re-elected Speaker, was largely due to Gingrich's efforts to bring down Democratic Speaker Jim Wright.

Just as the end balls of the parlor toy move the middle balls only negligibly as they batter them back and forth, we batter one another back and forth in unproductive conflict without significantly moving what stands between us. Yet no matter how hard the blows, gravity, sooner or later, gently brings the balls to rest. Similarly, no matter how long and hard we fight one another, sooner or later peace ensues. Just as perpetual motion is impossible, perpetual conflict is impossible. While the order of the universe is such that there will always be someone who will try to push us around—or at least we'll perceive that they are—it is also such that all conflict will end in peace. Even in the Middle East where conflict has seemed continuous for thousands of years, the periods of outright warfare have been relatively brief. Since Israel's 15-month war for independence in 1948, for example, there have been two full-scale wars, one of which lasted for six days and the other for three weeks (Hirsch 35, 38, 41, 42). Why, with all the hostile feelings in the Middle East, have the periods of war been relatively brief? Because it takes enormous amounts of energy and resources to carry on strife. Even well-trained boxers fight only three minutes between breaks. Litigants, too, know how much energy lawsuits consume. Lovers feel drained of energy when they fight. Sooner or later, their stamina sapped, combatants invariably breathe a heavy sigh and collapse in exhaustion. So why fight it? Since the forces of the universe inexorably move us toward peace, why fight them indeed?

Instead, let us flow with the forces of connection and peace, for the payoffs are enormous. Chapters 12 and 13 show how courage is not only the driving force of peace and human connection, but also of satisfying conflict resolution and productive work. We'll explore how courage enables us to make the shift from pseudo-community and chaos to emptiness, and through emptiness to community in the legal system, in the workplace, in intimate relationships, and among our institutions. Then, in Chapter 14, we'll examine the rewards.

CHAPTER 12

COURAGE IN THE LEGAL SYSTEM

Lawyers with Courage

In the early morning hours of May 17, 1990, a mammoth fireball seared the night air as a chemical-plant boiler blew apart, spewing toxic elements into the surrounding environment. From his suburban bedroom halfway across town, the plant foreman vomited upon realizing what had occurred: one of the largest environmental disasters of the century.

After spending billions on the clean-up, the chemical company sued its insurance company, which had denied coverage. Throughout the litigation, the insurance company lawyers behaved like their client—nastily. During the trial, the lead insurance company lawyer disobeyed the trial court's order to prevent certain irrelevant, prejudicial facts from coming into evidence. Ted Stanford, a lead lawyer for the chemical company, popped straight out of his chair and angrily exclaimed, within the jury's hearing, "You sonofabitch!"

The next day, the insurance company lawyer approached Stanford to say that he knew that he had really accomplished something when he'd been cussed by Ted Stanford in front of a jury.

While this might appear to be a joking attempt to get closer, I believe it was an attempt to flee from chaos into pseudo-community. There was no honest acknowledgment of wrongdoing, no taking of responsibility for violating the rules.

Nevertheless, Stanford responded by putting his hand on the insurance lawyer's shoulder and saying, "Conrad, I'm still angry about what you did, but I forgive you."

Stanford was courageous. Conrad had brazenly violated the rules at Stanford's expense. Stanford could have retaliated in kind by "accidentally" telling the jury things that the insurance company had gotten excluded from the evidence. And he certainly could have continued to blame Conrad—and with lots of self-righteousness, too. But, no, Stanford had the courage to empty himself of his desire to retaliate and to blame, and he forgave Conrad. He sought to move closer to him, and to connect.

Throughout the case, the chemical company's lawyers acted predominantly out of courage whereas the insurance company lawyers acted predominantly out of fear. The insurance company lawyers acted either unethically, as exemplified in Conrad's violation of the court's order, or with outright hostility. The incident in Chapter 2 in which the court admonished one of the lawyers who was about to fight with another to "back off and stand over here" occurred in this case, and it was an insurance company lawyer who was getting physical. Also, the insurance company lawyers repeatedly bad-mouthed the trial judge, both during the trial and after the verdict. They repeatedly tried to avoid going to trial, even attempting three times to move the case to federal court. Their negative demeanor was commented on by the jury in contrast to the highly positive feelings the jury had for the chemical-company lawyers. In the face of all of this, the chemical-company lawyers acted with restraint and stayed focused on their client's objectives.

Several weeks later, the chemical company won a $400 million verdict: every penny they asked for. What's more, they received a favorable answer on every question that was submitted to the jury.[37] By some accounts, the chemical company had a much stronger case than the insurance company. And its lawyers also enjoyed more favorable

[37] Civil juries in Texas render verdicts by answering questions about the facts of the case put to them by the trial judge.

COURAGE IN THE LEGAL SYSTEM

treatment from the trial judge—or so the insurance-company lawyers claimed. It thus might be argued that it's easier to be courageous when you have a strong position. True enough. However, there's a chicken-and-egg question here: Does courage makes our position strong, or does a strong position give us courage? Regardless of which comes first, courage makes for a strong position. If the insurance company really did have a weak case, that meant it owed the claim. Instead of trying to justify a weak position and blame the chemical company, it could have taken responsibility for its initial refusal to pay, apologized, and offered payment. Had it done so during the mediations that occurred, the chemical-company lawyers acknowledge that the case could have settled for far less than the insurance company was ultimately assessed.

The moral of this story? *Courage is powerful.* Even when the insurance-company lawyers repeatedly engaged in hostile, justify/blame behavior, the chemical-company lawyers had the courage not to respond in kind, but to remain focused on their client's objectives. It takes a great deal of courage to meet relentless hostility with restraint. And there is nothing more powerful than a lawyer's single-minded quest to ascertain the responsibility for a wrong without being distracted along the way by who is up and who is down.

But what if the other side incorrigibly engages in lying or other repugnant behavior like the master of attrition in Chapter 4, or the lying wife-beater in Chapter 1, or like Mr. Pelo? Courage in such a situation means focusing steadfastly on our ultimate objective. We do not need to hate or fear such opponents to do what is necessary to achieve desired results. Courage means staying centered.

In the case of the wife-beater (Chapter 1), there was no need to be hostile or show disrespect to him. The focus was simply to expose the truth. In the case of someone like the master of attrition, there is no need for an opposing lawyer to become hostile. There is no need to "show Pelo that he's not going to get away with that sort of behavior." It is only necessary, with our focus on our ultimate objective, to offer such lawyers choices that encourage them to be responsible: "You are certainly free to do what you are doing and say what you are saying. I would like, though, to let you know what I intend to do if you persist, so that you can make an informed choice." Those of us who have reared children may recognize this restrained and grownup technique. We recognize that we cannot directly control anyone, not even our children, much less other lawyers. What we can do is create circumstances that encourage them to choose to be responsible. Letting go of the false security of control is courageous—a product of emptiness and being centered.

Not only were the chemical-company lawyers successful in trial, but their refusal to engage in hostility made it easier to approach settling the case before all the appeals were exhausted. The additional distance that hostility creates did not have to be bridged before the parties shifted to a cooperative settlement mode. While the parties may have been in pseudo-community when the matter settled, at least they did not have to overcome additional hostility to get there.

A friend of mine recently represented an insurance company in the mediation of a case in which the plaintiff was claiming significant damages from serious personal injuries. In the opening statements, another of the insurance-company lawyers stated that the plaintiff was partly culpable for his own injuries. After separating the parties and meeting with the plaintiff and his lawyer, the mediator told the insurance-company group that the plaintiff was willing to settle for $700,000, or, if the insurance-company group would take back calling the plaintiff "culpable," the plaintiff would offer to settle for $650,000. My friend then asked the mediator to find out how much the plaintiff would settle for if "we called him 'precious'?" From then on, the tenor of the negotiations lightened, as the parties humorously parried back and forth to tell "precious" this and ask "precious" that. The plaintiff, clearly disarmed by this humoring, ended up agreeing to take significantly less than he had originally requested and than the insurance company would have paid.

My friend resisted the temptation to respond in kind to what many lawyers would have considered a challenge, a provocation. Instead of getting hung up on whether the plaintiff was culpable—who was right about that and who was wrong—she moved closer to the defendants by emptying herself of the urges to get hostile and making an accommodating, albeit humorous, response.

Courageous Litigants

Most lawsuits end when the parties stop the chaos and retreat into pseudo-community long enough to record the agreement into which they have beaten each other. On the other hand, they sometimes move through emptiness to the point of community. Here's an example.

Jack just wanted to help. And that's why he volunteered himself and his Colt .45 semi-automatic pistol when his boss, Will, mentioned that he had to go to a man's house to recover an overcharge. Will said the man was very large and might be violent. Will was going to bring his pistol.

Van, the man he was going to see, was a building contractor who had done some work on Will's house. Will had accused Van of overcharging him.

*   *   *

Will's white truck eases up to the small frame house. Van is out front in his yard. Jack gets out of the pickup, stands behind it, and levels the .45 at Van. Will begins a heated discussion about the overcharges. Van asks Jack to put the gun down.

Van's wife, who has been diagnosed with heart problems, becomes hysterical as she arrives on the scene after coming from the side yard. Then Van's son suddenly appears at the door of the house with a rifle. Van orders him to put the gun down. He obeys. The "discussion" gets nowhere. Jack and the boss decide to leave. They are arrested a few blocks away. Jack pleads guilty to a misdemeanor firearms charge and is given probation.

*   *   *

Van files suit against Will and Jack for assault. Will settles, but Jack countersues for assault, based on the son's aiming the rifle at him. Van claims that the rifle was only a BB gun.

*　*　*

I'm the mediator. The case of Van and his family against Jack, and Jack's counterclaim against Van and his son, is set for trial in two weeks.

It becomes clear that this is not a case in which back and forth, tit-for-tat bargaining will work. Jack is judgment-proof. Although a court might award a judgment against him, Van would not be able to collect it because Jack has no assets that may be taken to satisfy a judgment.

In a private caucus during the mediation, Jack tells me that he is willing to offer $1,000. He is also genuinely sorry about what he has done.

Van is a mountain of a man, plain-spoken and genuinely distressed that his family was traumatized by Jack's conduct. He is also offended that Jack was only given probation. Van starts out asking for $10,000.

I explain that Jack is judgment-proof and that he is offering $1,000. I tell Van that although Jack has gotten probation, he has had to spend a considerable sum on a criminal lawyer and his probation has some burdensome requirements. I tell Van that Jack is genuinely sorry; that I've seen folks offer apologies in mediations that are manipulative but that I don't think that of Jack. Jack is willing to apologize man-to-man.

Van and his lawyer agree to accept Jack's offer. Van and Jack then meet face-to-face across my conference table. Except for me, they are alone.

Jack looks Van straight in the eye and starts out, *"I want you to know that I didn't even know you before all this began. All I was trying to do was to help my boss. This was nothing personal against you. I know that what I did was wrong; it was a real cowboy kind of thing to do, and I'm sorry that I hurt you and your family. I know that I would not like it if someone had done the same to me and my wife."*

Van responds, *"When a man says you owe him money, he's not supposed to come after you with a gun. If I owed him money he could have filed on me in court. My wife and my grandbaby who was in the yard still talk about that day. I thought I was dead. This isn't about the money. I've had a long time to think about that day and I don't really care about myself. All I really care about is my family and what they have been through."*

Jack says, still making direct eye contact, *"I'm really sorry for what I put your family through. I had no intention of doing that. Sometimes you do things and you look back on them and wonder, 'What possessed me to do that?' All I can say now is I'm 'sorry'."*

Van says simply, *"Apology accepted."* He talks about what the experience was like for him and his family. The two shake hands. Everyone leaves.

Several days later, letters from the lawyers express their own and their client's renewed faith in the justice system.

Although it took no courage to assault a man with a .45 automatic, it took courage for Jack to sincerely acknowledge his error. To transcend the chaos, Jack let go of his justifications, making it easier for Van to let go of his need to punish or avenge the wrong to his family. Had this been the more typical mediation, with tit-for-tat bargaining, the chaos would have either continued through a trial or, at mediation's end, Van would at best have walked away with the $1,000 but once again felt shafted by "the system." By emptying of his justifications and communicating that emptiness through his apology, Jack was able to let go of the matter. Both men walked away feeling good.

The way the matter ended will have a positive effect on how the two approach conflict in the future, unlike the result in Emma Wheeler's case (Chapter 6). Jack experienced the positive reinforcement of forgiveness when he acknowledged his responsibility. This will encourage him to own responsibility in the future. Van felt that he was heard and respected and that fair amends were made. He will not hold onto the anger from this event and act it out the next time he encounters someone in a more powerful position.

The shopping-mall case we discussed in Chapter 6 is another example of how courageous litigants can move from one phase to another. When Don approached Robert, the store manager, and began with small talk, the two were in pseudo-community. This was, for them, the "testing the waters" phase of interaction.

They quickly moved into chaos when Don made it clear that he wanted to change something about Robert and the Harvey's sporting-goods operation, and Robert and Harvey intended to resist. Most litigation stays in chaos with intermittent retreats into pseudo-community. As we have seen, the "pseudo" in pseudo-community often involves lying and other deception, and the chaos is characterized by attempts to persuade, manipulate, control, and prevail over another, coupled with resistance and retaliation.

Unlike most litigants who shuffle back and forth between chaos and pseudo-community, Don and Harvey experienced emptiness. They let go of the need to try to manipulate and overpower one another. The apology by Don, followed by Harvey's responsive willingness to listen, moved them into community, the phase in which productive work could begin. Once they reached that point, they were able to effectively problem-solve. The key to getting there was voluntarily letting go of their internal barriers to productive communication.

A final example of courageous litigants reflects our enormous capacity for emptiness and forgiveness:

Two members of the United Klans of America took it upon themselves to avenge the death of a white policeman by murdering the first convenient black man they came upon. Nineteen-year-old Michael Donald was in the wrong place at the wrong time. He was later found with his face battered, his throat slit—and hung by the neck.

The two killers were eventually caught and convicted. James "Tiger" Knowles and Henry Hayes were sentenced to long prison terms. But the responsibility of the Klan for instigating the murder was yet to be addressed.

The Southern Poverty Law Center, a non-profit champion of civil rights, brought a civil suit against the Klan and the individual Klansmen responsible for the murder of

Michael Donald. After an hour-and-a-half of deliberations, the jury awarded $7 million in damages to the mother of Michael Donald. Although the Klan's assets amounted to but a fraction of the award, it had to deed its headquarters to Mrs. Donald. Reflecting on the trial, Morris Dees, the founder of the Southern Poverty Law Center and lead trial lawyer for Mrs. Donald, described the following events:

"I think one of the most memorable and dramatic moments that I've ever had in a courtroom was at the end of the Donald trial. I finished my closing argument and the Klan lawyer had finished his, and James Knowles, one of the defendants, stood up and asked the judge if he could say something to the jury. He walked over in front of the jury and he said, *'Everything that Mr. Dees said we did, we did. We did it at the direction of those Klansmen sitting right over there—those leaders.'* And he turned to Mrs. Donald and said, *'Mrs. Donald, now, I've lost everything that I ever had in my life—my home, my family, I'm in prison for life. I'd like to ask you if you could find it in your heart to forgive me.'* And she kind of rocked back in her chair, looked at him in front of that jury, and said, *'Son, I've already forgiven you.'* There wasn't a dry eye in that courtroom—at our counsel table, in that jury box, and even on the bench. This old woman, who had lost her son, one of the most precious things in her life, was able to reach out to that teenage Klansman, who was himself a victim of racism and prejudice, and forgive him. It was a love that we hear so much about but know so little of. Her words in that courtroom that day were a higher justice than that $7 million verdict from that jury. And I thought to myself, *'If that could be transcended out of the courtroom, that love, that understanding of people who are different from each other, if we could change the hearts and minds of people of all races and religions and cultures, both black and white and others in this country, if we could teach tolerance and understanding, then we might could prevent future Michael Donalds and prevent future killings....'"* [38]

[38] Excerpted from promotional video produced by the Southern Poverty Law Center, Montgomery, Alabama.

The Klansman, James Knowles, had pled guilty and taken responsibility for his part in the brutal crime. He apparently had emptied himself of the hate of a lifetime and humbled himself in front of a woman whose son he had apparently not even been able to see as a person. By forgiving her son's murderer, Mrs. Donald had emptied herself of the rage any mother would have felt in the circumstances. The influence of her courage will carry far beyond that courtroom. Consider how differently the telling of this story would affect the cause of racial harmony had Mrs. Donald not summoned the courage to forgive.

This sequence of acceptance of responsibility followed by forgiveness casts a resplendent gleam on the human spirit. As witnesses to such miracles, we find comfort in the knowledge that we can fail in the most profound ways and still find forgiveness and redemption. This revelation creates room within us to forgive our own failings, which in turn enables us to accept what we see as failings in others. When we approach one another from our centers with such emptiness, we are radiant.

CHAPTER 13

COURAGE IN LIFE

All of us have roles we play. We may be, at various times, workers, supervisors, parents, children, leaders, followers, lovers, friends. And of course we may encounter conflict in any of these roles. When we do, our courage is on trial. We can continue trying to resolve conflict in ways that we've grown comfortable with and which offer only illusory peace, or we can teach ourselves to first focus on acknowledging our *own* contributions to it through emptiness and responsibility, and grow closer together.

In the last chapter, we looked at courage in our roles as clients and lawyers. Here, we look at what courage means in our other roles.

Courage in the Workplace

All organizations have cultures or unspoken principles of operation. Some organizational cultures pay lip service to the principle of community; others embrace it, but even they resist it more than they sometimes realize. Why? Because people find it far easier to retreat from chaos into pseudo-community than to go through emptiness into community. This section is about striving for community in organizations that resist it.

What issues face management when seeking to instill the principles of courage in the workplace? Let me offer, as a case study, the experience of my own law firm. After attending several Community Building Workshops[39] during 1992 and 1993, I informally put one on for my staff hoping to introduce them to the process of moving from

[39] Dr. Peck has set up an organization that conducts such workshops. It's called the Foundation for Community Encouragement. See "Epilogue," *infra*.

one phase to the other, particularly from chaos to emptiness. The experience initially proved quite painful for the group as several of us were confronted with unpleasant truths about ourselves. The ultimate payoff, especially for one employee, and in turn, for the firm, was extraordinary. That employee had long held herself apart from us. Instead of recognizing any personal responsibility for the overall welfare of our office, she saw herself as responsible solely for doing her own job, as she narrowly defined it. In effect, she worked in a cocoon. When, during our "workshop," one after another of our employees let her know how her attitude and behavior affected them, she felt deeply rejected. But eventually she summoned the courage to acknowledge her part in creating their reactions. At that point, she began to let go of her barriers to being a responsible member of the team. She developed a new sense of loyalty and, for the first time at our office, participated in mutual cooperation. As she moved closer to the rest of us, our whole office began to communicate far more openly and develop a healthy work environment.

But maintaining that environment takes work, too. It's easy to backslide. My own group has had difficulty maintaining effective conflict-resolution processes because of distractions. I myself am hardly immune to them. Like many executives, I have numerous things competing for my time—my clients, my family, my professional and spiritual development, my community service, my writing... Several years ago, some staffmembers told me that when they needed to talk to me, I often greeted them with "the look," which, when I became conscious of it, I realized was an irritated glare. They interpreted "the look" to mean "I resent your interrupting me"—and they were right. I often felt that my own work was too important for me to deal with a distracting staffmember who needed my attention. Once I realized how important my attention was to the health of our work environment, I stopped resenting the interruptions and instead saw them as an essential part of my management function.

Another reason that we've found it hard to maintain our community is that we've been tempted, like many organizations, to deal with building community and resolving conflict in much the same way as many Americans deal with physical fitness. Just as people jump from fad diet to fad diet and workout gadget to workout gadget, always looking for a miracle cure, organizations tend to jump from one training program to the next. What organization, for example, has not had its "visioning" sessions or weekend retreats devoted to drafting a mission statement? There are thousands of workshops and consultants in today's marketplace, all offering valuable but limited services. These processes raise our consciousness, yes, but they cannot instill the courage that it takes to make lasting change. That must come from within the organization and must be ongoing, with a zealous commitment to the continuous process.

To expect our organizations to maintain community and effectively resolve conflict after just one workshop or "visioning" session would be like telling the 90-pound weakling to take on the beach bully after a single workout. An organization needs time and exercise to develop the "muscle" that will enable it to continuously empty. And managers leading such organizations must not only be able to train others in the fitness techniques but must model them as well. If they don't, their integrity will be rightly questioned and their credibility undermined.

Ever since the workshop, our office has experienced recurrences of all four stages of human relationship. We've found that we must actively monitor our behavior—not to avoid any stage, but to constantly move toward connection with one another. For without that vigilance, we slip into pseudo-community, where wounds fester until they explode into chaos. Of course, when they do, we must work to do the necessary emptying to return to community. We have found that courage is not only the *willingness* to experience community, but also the *will* to pursue it—constantly. Such courage is required because we often fear allowing others to be close to us.

Courage in management requires the discipline to incessantly develop one's own consciousness and to strive toward being in community with the members of the organization. It also requires the discipline to continually develop the capacity within other members of the organization to do the same. This can be done not only by sending them to workshops and encouraging their own personal growth, but also by personally modeling empty behavior.

On the other hand, nothing is a greater enemy of community than trying to "fix" people who "don't do it right" or who resist. Some may not be comfortable with the same level of self-disclosure or honesty as those who have more experience with community; some may be more comfortable with their thoughts than their feelings; some may just not want as much intimacy as others. Ironically, as managers, we must empty of our need for changing them in order to be in community with them. When we accept their differences, we move closer to them.

At a leadership workshop I attended recently, I met a young woman named Sally, who was a mid-level executive in a company owned by an overbearing boss. His verbal abuse so flustered her, she confessed, that she felt powerless to deal with him effectively.

The trainers leading the workshop suggested to her that we do a workplace role-play simulation. I agreed to play her overbearing boss. The context we were given was an annual discussion about the organization of the company's four divisions, one of which she headed. The other division chiefs—also played by workshop participants—were also in the room. All acted totally cowed by the boss and unsupportive of Sally.

"Sally, I'd like to hear about your plans for the organization of your division," I began.

"I think Ginny deserves to be promoted to section chief," she replied.

"Well, that's not gonna work," I said, matter-of-factly. *"Ginny won't be able to take control of that section. Her family situation has kept her from being a true team player. You need to rethink that decision."*

"I've thought about this very carefully, Mark," she asserted. *"Despite her family commitments, she works just as hard as the other section chiefs. And, besides, she has the respect of all the employees in that section."*

"Goddammit," I retorted with flame-thrower eyes, as I slammed my notebook on the ground and menacingly shot from my chair, *"I said 'you need to rethink that decision.' Didn't you hear me the first time?"*

"I really don't agree, Richard," she said, unconsciously using her boss's real name. *"I really feel strongly about this,"* she added bravely, but shaken. She was now on her feet.

I stalked across the room until I was six inches from her face. I was beside myself, shouting now: *"I'm not asking much from you. All I want is a little gratitude and respect. I'm good to my employees. Now I'm gonna ask you one more goddam time: Are you gonna rethink that decision?"*

Here, the trainer intervened and took Sally's place in the role play. He was a powerful man. I felt my adrenalin surging as he stared back at me. I repeated my question: *"Are you gonna rethink that decision?"*

The trainer turned aside and began to try to involve the other "division chiefs": *"Do you guys see what's happening here? Do you really want to work under..."*

I cut him off. *"Don't you dare talk to them! This is between you and me. They got nothin' to do with this. You guys get the hell outta here. I'm gonna finish this. All I want is for you to say that you will rethink this decision."* I was almost screaming now.

"I'm gettin' a lawyer and gettin' outta here, and if you're smart, you will, too," he declared to Sally's mute colleagues.

"You can get whatever you want but you're not working for me unless you rethink your decision," I concluded, red-faced and shrieking.

The trainer ended the exercise there, and we had a group discussion about what had happened. One woman admitted that she'd gotten so caught up in the drama that she almost came out of her chair and entered the fray. She later said that she had been victimized by someone like the character I portrayed.

After the discussion, I spoke to Sally and told her what it was like to portray her boss. I told her how fearful I had been the entire time—afraid of being bested, first by her and then by the trainer. The more confrontational she got, even in her gentle way, the more it set me off. When the trainer started in, my fear level shot up and my voice elevated accordingly. I experienced a deep fear of humiliation, of losing. What was good for the company was *not* the issue once we engaged. All I cared about was not losing.

The next day, Sally stood up to speak to the other participants of the workshop. Her feet were anchored. Her posture was erect and powerful. Her center of gravity was low in her abdomen. She was unshakable. Her voice was firm as she proclaimed, "I am no longer afraid."

Realizing now that her boss was more afraid than she was, she was able to overcome her own fear and was prepared to meet him from her center—the abode of her courage. She could now resist the urge to run or to challenge him. And once the issue was no longer who was going to win and who was going to lose, she might be able to find an opening to work toward resolution of the original problem. And, as she put it later in a letter to me, "Perhaps after I learn to truly survive these types of incidents I may choose to extend myself for the spiritual growth of 'Richard'."

Some bosses may continue to be abusive, no matter how loving their employees. In such cases, resorting to the legal system or simply finding another job may be one's only real option. But in the majority of cases, how much more effective is Sally's courageous approach than the current fashion of Victim's Syndrome—continually blaming the boss rather than taking responsibility for resolving the conflict. By assuming that responsibility, Sally has the opportunity not only to develop a consensus decision with her boss on the underlying issue, but also to keep future decisions from degenerating into up-and-downsmanship. She has the opportunity to be genuinely powerful.

Courage operates similarly in any situation where one is structurally subordinate in a workplace power relationship. The subordinate must first take responsibility for finding a way out of the up-and-downsmanship.[40] This may take acknowledging the superior/subordinate rela-

---

[40] Ideally, the boss, who is in a superior position, should make the first move because it's easier to let go of power from a superior position than to exert power from a subordinate one.

tionship itself—saying, for example, "Of course, I recognize your managerial prerogatives and will support your final decisions as long as I work for you." Doing whatever it takes to eliminate what the boss fears is the first step. The second step is simply offering information that may be helpful to the boss in making the decision—saying, for example, "You may want to consider that if we fail to promote [Blank], she may quit and it will cost significant dollars to replace her," or "Our general counsel tells me that we need to be careful to avoid a discrimination claim."

Lots of us go to work every day hating our jobs because we feel disconnected from our co-workers, whether we consider them subordinates, superiors, or peers. We spend most of our waking hours in their company. In this world of alienation and disconnection, where we hardly know our neighbors anymore and family members are dispersed across the country, what an opportunity we have to create communities in our workplaces where we can support one another and thrive together in peace.

Courage with Loved Ones

A friend of mine who's a successful and aggressive lawyer-turned-businessman recently went through a divorce after more than 20 years of marriage. The circumstances had all the makings of a classic divorce war. The husband had amassed a multimillion-dollar fortune— more than enough to make it worthwhile for an angry spouse to hire a barracuda lawyer to fight for it, and more than enough to make a barracuda lawyer happy to fight. The wife, concerned about her financial security due to the husband's entrepreneurial tendencies, hired just such a lawyer—the most aggressive one she could find.

Fortunately, since the couple's children were grown, the only issue in the divorce was the property division. Knowing that property fights can be expensive and unproductive, and valuing his wife's friendship, the husband decided at the outset that his decisions concerning the division of property would be based solely on what would be beneficial to the health and welfare of himself *and his wife.*

During negotiations over the property, his wife's lawyer challenged him in several areas. In each case, he acknowledged the fairness of his wife's position without selling himself short. The matter was settled without any depositions being taken or any orders being issued—and no trial. He and his wife both ended up with "oodles" of money, as he put it, without having to pay exorbitant legal fees.

Much of the success of that settlement can be traced to my friend's resisting the urge to respond in kind to aggressive moves by his wife's lawyer. He had the courage to avoid lying and other repugnant behavior—and the payoff was enormous, particularly considering the alternative. Besides the monetary payoff to both of them, they managed to remain friends.

I can relate. I have often joked that I am better to be divorced from than to be married to because I get along so well with my two exes. During our divorces, both of my former wives and I resisted the urge to be hostile. We reached amicable settlements that we both felt good about. Today, I consider them both friends, and they consider me a friend as well. What's more, my first wife and I have raised two children who intuitively know the meaning of responsibility and emptiness. My college-age son has on several occasions offered unsolicited apologies when he has contributed to disconnections between us. When my daughter was 15, after two years of going through the obligatory "Dad is a dork" stage, she wrote the following message on my Father's Day card:

> Dear Dad,
> I know I haven't been the easiest teenager,
> but I had a lot of fun w/you yesterday.
> So I think I'm almost over that stage.

Although the process of separation and divorce often brings out the worst in us, it doesn't have to be that way. Divorce is typically fraught with justification and blame that are more intense than in any other kind of litigation. However, there are many of us, men and women alike, who accept responsibility for our part of the conflict and empty of the hostility that bred the failure of the marriage. We have the power to choose courage over fear.

Moreover, the choice we make will have momentous consequences for those we hold dear. Just as children model the behavior of their parents, the way we adults handle the conflict that breeds and is acted out in divorce will be a model for conflict resolution that will be visited upon all of our children, for better or worse.

Even in families that don't experience divorce, the way in which parents handle conflict will have a dominant influence on how their own children handle it. If we adults engage in continual chaotic verbal assaults, our children may emulate the "screaming and yelling" model of conflict resolution because that's all they know. Or they may eschew intimate relationships altogether because they fear suffering the fate of their tormented role models.

The effects of continually fleeing from chaos into pseudo-community may be just as pernicious as those from being mired in chaos. Our children may learn to harbor resentments, to be disingenuous, and to be outright deceptive.

But when we adults take responsibility for our part in conflict, we show our children how to achieve satisfaction and intimacy in relationships. Not only can we heal our own relationships, but we can raise an evolved generation capable of the kind of connection that we may only imagine.

Institutional Courage

We have already spoken of chaos within ourselves and between embattled lawyers representing their clients. Interestingly, those same relationship dynamics exist among institutions as well as between institutions and individuals. Whether the institutions are neighborhood groups or nation-states, the same principles still apply. Unfortunately our institutions have only rarely experienced community. Take, for example, our political parties. During World War II, they briefly came together to face a common enemy, achieving community of the type that occurs around natural disasters, but otherwise they've brought us interminable chaos, punctuated by rare moments of pseudo-community during the ever-shortening "honeymoon" periods following presidential elections.

Many other of our institutions are in chaos, too, both within themselves and between one another. A common reason is that our leaders don't seem to know how to act with courage. If our institutions are to move toward peace with one another, our leaders must be courageous representatives of them. How? By being willing to acknowledge their own contribution to the chaos, by creating the space for healing. The aim of this section is to offer concrete examples of courageous institutional messages.

I hesitate to write it, though, because it's one thing to acknowledge my own contributions to conflict and quite another to suggest that others acknowledge theirs. That said, let me offer the following not as a prescription but as an enzyme—something that may help our institutions digest their own messages of courage and enlightenment.

America's legal profession today, both within itself and in its relationship to laymen and other institutions, epitomizes chaos. Lawyers are joked about, scapegoated, and trashed by all segments of society. The very fact that people will buy a book called *Why Lawyers (and the Rest of Us) Lie and Engage in Other Repugnant Behavior* is fresh evidence that the legal system inspires more chaos than it knows what to do with.

But when people complain of our lying and other repugnant behavior, must we stay in chaos? Must we, with knee-jerk predictability, resist the pressures toward revolution with still more justifying and blaming? I think the legal profession has an opportunity to lead the revolution rather than be another of its casualties. We have an opportunity to say to our fellow Americans:

> As lawyers, we take responsibility for our lying and
> other repugnant behavior. We truly know the pain
> of deception, hostility, and alienation because we
> suffer with it day by day at the same time that we

profit by it. We commit, then, to making the difficult journey in a new direction: the direction of peace. We offer our community the gift of our example.

This message comes from emptiness. It leaves nothing to bash or push against. By taking responsibility, we stop the justify/blame dynamics that perpetuates lawyer-bashing as well as the unproductive conflict that drives the civil-justice system itself.

In 1996, America's Jews had an opportunity for institutional emptiness when the Southern Baptist Convention passed a resolution to try to convert them. This resolution, which came from a place of chaos, was an attempt to "fix" us Jews—to turn us into proper Baptists. Not surprisingly, the resolution provoked a furor among Jewish leaders. To them, this proclamation had an all-too-familiar ring. Throughout history, others have sought to obliterate not only the ways we Jews are different, but our very existence. So, many Jewish leaders rejected the Baptist overtures out of hand. Their net effect was to leave the religions further apart than ever.

But had we Jews had the courage to let go of fears of persecution, we might have been able to see the Baptist overtures as an attempt to move closer to us, although not necessarily in a way we would like. A response from emptiness might have been:

> We too have a desire to be closer to you. We do not want to allow our fears, born from thousands of years of persecution, to interfere with that. We respect your right to worship as you do, and we ask only the same in return. We would like to learn to appreciate your uniqueness. We would like to know more about your religion and culture so that we may understand you better, and we offer you the same opportunity to learn about ours. We seek to be in community with you.

Leading

As leaders, we often face a tension between the need to maintain the loyalty of our followers, which might be served by acting out their hostile urges, and the need to honor our own values of restraint and peace-making. As a lawyer, I face this tension whenever clients come to my office wanting blood—which is often. Admittedly, I sometimes feel the need to stand up for them, to be their champion, even if it means taking highly aggressive action. In my younger days, I sometimes unconsciously allowed the aggression to feed on itself without recognition that it was only a means rather than an end. But now when I act aggressively, it is with consciousness of an objective, and with constant probing for an opening to make peace. By meeting my clients where they are and then moving with them toward peace, I avoid getting oppositional with them and I maintain my own integrity.

Similarly, whether we are leaders of our families, large corporations, political parties, religions, or professions, we all may face the tension between our followers' thirst for combat and our own values of peace-making. Sometimes, courage demands a delicate sense of balance.

CHAPTER 14

THE REWARDS OF
COURAGE

For me, courage is its own reward. But I'm no martyr, and I confess that it would be difficult to stick by my principles if doing so constantly brought painful consequences. As it turns out, I've learned that courage generates not only intrinsic rewards, but extrinsic rewards as well.

Courage and Strength in Conflict

One extrinsic reward is strength in conflict. In Chapter 3 we saw the effectiveness of clean hands: being free of deceit and hostility ourselves, we stand before our judges in stark contrast to those who are not. We know from our discussion at the end of Chapter 10 that when we practice integrity, we not only bring people closer, but we also enhance our persuasiveness. Similarly, when we are centered and empty, free of our fear of losing, like a master of martial arts we are powerful adversaries. In his book *In Search of Atticus Finch: A Motivational Book for Lawyers*, based on Harper Lee's *To Kill a Mockingbird*, Mike Papantonio describes a passage in which Finch is spat upon by a racist. Finch responds by wiping his face and refusing to lower himself with a response in kind (34). Only later, he says that he wishes that the man didn't chew tobacco. Papantonio then compares Atticus Finch, the archetypal courageous lawyer, with his modern-day nemesis:

> ...[A]tticus' power is found in his restraint. The "in your face" approach to trial practice that has been evolving since the early seventies no doubt would

have been an annoyance to him, but the contentious, combative trial lawyer of the nineties
would be easy pickings for brother Finch. (35)

If courage is so effective, then how do we explain the
extraordinary financial success of lawyers like some of
those whose hostile handiwork we saw in Chapters 2 and
3? The answer does not lie in the behavior of the hostile
lawyer but in the behavior of the opposition.

How is the opposition likely to behave in the face of
hostility? As we saw in Part I, provocations result in a
response-in-kind and inevitable escalation. In fact, the
very success of hostile tactics *depends on baiting the opponent*—recall the lesson of wrestling with a pig. This means
that the hostile person's success depends on a response-in-
kind. Suppose, for example, a defendant has been negligent—say, by violating regulations of the Occupational
Safety and Health Administration (OSHA)—causing serious burn injuries to an employee. The defendant expects a
lawsuit. In order to minimize any claims for intangible
damages like pain and mental anguish, disfigurement, and
physical impairment, the defendant plans to apologize,
acknowledge responsibility, and pay the medical bills
immediately. This strategy will minimize the likelihood
that a jury would award huge damages.

Now, enter a Mr. Pelo. He sends an obnoxious letter
accusing the defendant of everything short of war crimes,
and all of a sudden, the defendant is provoked and no
longer feels conciliatory. In fact, the defendant gets so
angry that it cuts off the medical payments, denies violating the OSHA regulations, and now claims that the pitiful
plaintiff brought the injury upon himself. Now the defendant has given a jury something to avenge—by awarding
huge damages.

On the other hand, if the defendant had followed
through on its original plans, the hostility of the plaintiff's
lawyer wouldn't have made any difference. In fact, it
would only have hurt the plaintiff's lawyer.

Highly ethical plaintiffs' lawyers acknowledge that we
"cannot get a good verdict, a high verdict, without help

from the opposition" (Spivey). Large verdicts, then, are not a measure of the success of the hostile or unethical lawyer but of the failure of the opponent to be responsible.

Courage Prevents Future Conflict

All of us have a stake in the courageous resolution of conflict. Jurors in personal-injury cases are often keenly aware that the damage awards they make at least remotely affect all of us. They're spreading the cost of an injury from the victim of the accident to the insurance industry, which in turn passes the cost right along to the consumer. The cost of litigation also is borne by all of us through our tax dollars to support the civil-justice system. Each year, unproductive conflict costs untold sums. On the other hand, the only thing that protects each of us from being an uncompensated victim of someone else's carelessness is our willingness to award just compensation to our neighbors. The point is, the way every conflict is resolved may affect all of us.

This phenomenon of interconnectedness is sometimes lost on us lawyers and our clients. I've often heard litigants, lawyers, and even mediators say that unless there's an ongoing relationship between the litigants that is independent of the litigation, such as two divorcing spouses with children or two business partners, it doesn't really matter how the parties feel about each other at the end of the case. But if we leave litigants feeling like Emma Wheeler and her insurance adjusters, we've done little to prevent future conflict—and we'll all pay for it, either by being directly involved in conflict with one of the parties or by bearing the cost of that party's conflicts. For example, we may bear the cost of direct conflict if we have occasion to make a claim against Emma's insurance company, which will now feel fresh grounds for suspecting us of making an unfair claim, whether we deserve it or not. Indirectly, we may pay higher premiums to that company because they drive up the cost of litigation with their undue suspicion, and we may pay for their use of the courthouse with tax dollars. But if we have the courage to resolve conflict in community, we train ourselves to avoid future unproductive conflict.

Courage Produces Satisfying Conflict Resolution

Only when each of us has the courage to take responsibility for our part of the conflict, and thereby reach community, can both parties walk away from the conflict feeling satisfied with the outcome. We saw Jack and Van do this in the assault case, as did the landlord and tenant in the shopping-center case. The associate in my lawfirm also found the courage to be responsible for her barriers to being a team member and has since had a flourishing career.

When we are fearful, we deceive, engage in hostility, justify our own questionable conduct, and blame others. This provokes similar responses, which in turn lead to a spiral of escalation and may necessitate the intervention of a third-party decision-maker. Courage enables us both to avoid the cost of prolonged chaos and to *choose* the terms of resolution rather than have them forced upon us.

Courage Reduces the Cost of Conflict

The day-to-day, even moment-to-moment, choice of whether to distance the opposition or to bring them closer is the most important choice lawyers make that influences the cost of resolving the dispute. The more hostility that occurs, the more letting go will be necessary before resolution may be approached. Consider the case of my client Henry.

———————————

Henry owns 40% of the stock in a small corporation. Until last week, he was also employed by the company as its chief operating officer. At that time, the other shareholder, the 60% owner, fired him and made it clear that Henry would receive no dividends from the company, even though the company is very profitable. I suggest that we negotiate a sale of my client's shares to the majority shareholder. Our bargaining leverage is that so long as we don't get any money from the company, it'll be difficult for the majority shareholder to take money out of the company for himself, because he would have difficulty justifying to a court that he was getting a dividend while other shareholders were not. If the majority owner owns it all, on the other hand, he can control the company without our interference. But we can bring suit to try to force the majority shareholder to return some money that we believe he has illegally withdrawn from the company.

Henry insists that the majority owner will never be fair in a buyout negotiation unless we're aggressive. I tell him that we won't really know that until we try to negotiate. Angry and convinced that the majority shareholder won't be fair, Henry chooses to file suit.

Bob, the opposing lawyer, is someone I have dealt with over many years. He is very professional. He is also meticulous and perceived by some as difficult to work with. Despite our previous dealings, we manage, this time, to get very angry with each other. It is all I can do to keep the conflict from escalating out of control. When I have not given him certain documents on the day I have promised, he accuses me of hiding them. Actually, I haven't given him the documents on time simply through an oversight. Because we have begun settlement discussions, I have focused on them rather than on producing the documents. For a while I'm furious at his accusation. Then I realize that he believes that the real reason for my delay is that the documents are damaging to my client, not that I would like to settle the case before spending the time and money to assemble them. So I produce the documents as quickly as possible and apologize for missing the deadline.

After I have billed my client $18,000 in legal fees, we settle the case. The majority shareholder agrees to pay $150,000 for my client's stock, and a closing date is set. We also agree to dismiss our lawsuit before that date. But, as it turns out, Henry has lost the original stock certificates and cannot produce them at closing. Bob insists on receiving them before paying the money. Furious, Henry believes that the majority shareholder is just trying to get out of the deal, now that we have dismissed our lawsuit and lost our leverage. "Trust me on this one," I tell him. "Bob will cooperate if we will. He just wants to be sure that the shares have not been transferred to someone else who may make a claim against the company."

Bob and I work out a complex arrangement that protects his client despite Henry's inability to account for the original share certificates. We close the deal. Henry gets his money.

———————————

There were at least three critical forks in the road here. The first was when Henry chose to file suit rather than attempt negotiations. I think he made that choice out of fear. He believed that the majority shareholder had continually taken advantage of him and that he needed to show that he wouldn't allow that to happen again. In short, he feared being overpowered. This choice cost him $18,000 in legal fees. Granted, sometimes it's necessary to make an aggressive response before cooperating, especially if a cooperative move will be perceived as weak. And, admittedly, there are some people who invariably refuse to be fair until forced. We must exercise caution, however, before we make such assumptions, for they're often projections or based on unreliable predictors. If the aggressive response is conscious and aims at a speedy resolution of the conflict rather than at punishing the opponent, it may be courageous. But such action must always be consciously examined because it's fatally easy to rationalize aggression. To this day, I don't know whether Henry and I could have negotiated for a $150,000 price for the stock without filing suit. But I still think it would have cost the client far less than $18,000 to find out.

The second fork in the road was when I apologized for failing to produce the documents on time. Taking responsibility for my part in creating conflict removed this barrier to the beginning of serious settlement talks. Had we continued to fight about the documents, we would have lost sight of our objectives—for me, to get Henry a fair price for his stock; and for the opposing attorney, to end the litigation and remove Henry from his client's company.

The third fork in the road occurred when we chose not to file suit again after Bob insisted on seeing the original stock certificates. Again, we chose to own responsibility for our part of the problem (not producing the original certificates), and the problem was resolved.

Consider the difference that other choices would have made in Henry's case. Had he attempted negotiation before filing suit, he might have saved thousands in legal fees. Had Bob and I stayed locked in the document dispute, Henry would have been charged thousands more.

Civil conflict can end after a single exchange of letters or phone calls and the expenditure of a few hundred dollars in legal fees. Or it can proceed through a trial, two or three appeals, retrial, protracted bankruptcy, and the expenditure of thousands—sometimes even millions—of dollars in legal fees. At some point, all disputes end. Moreover, they all end when both sides have finished fighting. How long cases take to be resolved and how much they cost to be resolved depends on whether lawyers move toward peace or toward war: fundamentally, on whether we are courageous or fearful.

Consider the way litigation proceeds under the competitive game assumption that was discussed in Chapter 3, as opposed to how it proceeds under the cooperative game assumption:

Competitive: We will use every means permitted by the rules of procedure to prevail over the opposition.

vs.

Cooperative: We will exchange sufficient information to enable us each to evaluate the case, make good-faith efforts to settle, and, failing that, afford one another a fair opportunity to present the case on the merits.

If, under the competitive assumption, the lawsuit is viewed as a "case to be tried," all efforts push the parties further and further apart, resulting in spiraling escalation. But if, on the other hand, the lawsuit is viewed as a dispute to be resolved, as it is under the cooperative game assumption, all efforts focus on moving the parties closer, and the costs of conflict are minimized.

But what about conflicts outside the legal system? If we apply to them the cooperative game assumption that we have been exploring in the legal context, this is how it might read:

We will exchange sufficient information to enable us to evaluate our positions, *acknowledge our own responsibility for contributing to the problem,* make good-faith efforts to resolve the conflict, and, failing that, afford one another a fair opportunity for hearing before a neutral third party.

Think how much more effectively we could resolve conflict! And were we to add the italicized phrase, think how much aggravation we could save!

Courage Is an Essential Attribute of Competence

How important is courage to being a competent lawyer? I used to think that the courage to make peace and connect with the opposition was necessary only in family-law matters, where the parties would usually have an ongoing relationship, especially if they had children. In fact, when someone would ask me for a referral to a family lawyer, the first question I'd ask was, "Who's representing the spouse?" I'd then recommend a lawyer who would get along well with the opposing lawyer. My theory was that while we had divorce lawyers aplenty who were technically competent, the key to a satisfactory divorce settlement lay in finding a lawyer who also had the ability to find ways to make peace. I now believe that the courage to make peace and connect with the opposition is an essential attribute of any competent lawyer, regardless of the case.

In selecting a lawyer, clients should consider asking about the lawyer's approach to litigation. If he or she carries the reputation of being a "hired gun" (or a "barracuda" or some other such metaphor), the client is likely to get a one-dimensional approach and can count on high bills and unproductive conflict. This lawyer is likely to be able to boast of spectacular wins. What you won't hear about are the equally spectacular defeats.

If, on the other hand, the lawyer tells you something like the following, you will probably have more than a one-trick pony:

We view litigation as sometimes necessary if other, more cost-effective strategies fail. We first look for cooperative strategies to encourage the assumption of responsibility and to resolve conflict. If you have truly exhausted those, we can certainly litigate. And if they want a fight, we know how to do that effectively.

Sometimes you'll hear yet another philosophy, which runs something like this: "We don't believe in litigation; we think all cases should be settled through mediation." Such a lawyer may prove too weak to make the hard choices necessary to encourage the other side to take responsibility for their part of the problem.

Courage Is Healthy

The capsule description of "Type A" behavior that appears on the cover of the 1970s best-seller, *Type A Behavior and Your Heart*, by Drs. Meyer Friedman and Ray Rosenman, characterizes someone in chaos with himself and others:

A special, well-defined pattern marked by a compelling sense of time urgency—"hurry sickness"—aggressiveness and competitiveness, usually combined with a marked amount of free-floating hostility. Type A's engage in a chronic, continuous struggle against circumstances, against others, against themselves. The behavior pattern is common among hard-driving and successful businessmen and executives—but is just as likely to be found in factory workers, accountants, even housewives. About half of all American males—and a growing number of females—are more or less confirmed Type A's.

People stuck in Type A behavior are people who, by definition, do not reach emptiness and community. Unfortunately, "more than 90% of the people having heart attacks prior to the age of seventy are Type A's" (Papantonio 33). Although the *Type A Behavior* book proved enormously influential, and though it gives us a wonderful metaphor for people living in chaos, its conclusions have been substantially refined.

In recent years, researchers have learned that it is not the hurried, high-pressure existence of Type A personalities that is associated with heart disease so much as it's the hostility. Daniel Goleman, in his acclaimed work *Emotional Intelligence*, catalogues the significant findings:

- In a Stanford University Medical School study, a group of heart patients was asked to recount incidents that made them angry, the object being to see if anger might significantly affect heart function. "The effect was striking," Goleman observed. "[W]hile the patients recounted incidents that made them mad, the pumping efficiency of their hearts dropped by five percentage points. Some of the patients showed a drop in pumping efficiency of 7 percent or greater—a range that cardiologists regard as a sign of a myocardial ischemia, a dangerous drop in blood flow to the heart itself."
- Dr. Redford Williams at Duke University "found that those physicians who had had the highest scores on a test of hostility while still in medical school were seven times as likely to have died by the age of fifty as were those with low hostility scores—being prone to anger was a stronger predictor of dying young than were other risk factors such as smoking, high blood pressure, and high cholesterol."
- "Dr. John Barefoot at the University of North Carolina, show[ed] that in heart patients undergoing angiography, in which a tube is inserted into the coronary artery to measure lesions, scores on a test of hostility correlated with the extent and severity of coronary artery disease."
- "[A] Yale...study of 929 men who had survived heart attacks and were tracked for up to ten years" showed that "[t]hose who had been rated as easily roused to anger were three times more likely to die of cardiac arrest than those who were more even-tempered."

- "A Harvard Medical School study asked more than fifteen hundred men and women who had suffered heart attacks to describe their emotional state in the hours before the attack. Being angry more than doubled the risk of cardiac arrest in people who already had heart disease; the heightened risk lasted for about two hours after the anger was aroused." (169-171)

For those of us in a profession in which hostility is a way of life, these are sobering findings. Indeed, to the extent that lawyers are engaged in prolonged conflict, they face an elevated risk of heart attacks ("Exhaustion" 784).

What, then, is the antidote? Trying to suppress our anger won't work. It may actually magnify the body's agitation and increase blood pressure (Goleman 171). And just venting our anger won't work, either. That simply feeds it and makes it "a more likely response to any annoying situation." Instead, Goleman's advice, based on medical research, is to be particularly conscious of anger as it arises, regulate it once it has begun, and be empathetic (171).

We've seen these steps before. Being conscious of emotions, including anger, is the first step toward courage in conflict. When we "regulate" our anger, we are centering. And when we have empathy, we move closer to others. Courage enlivens not only the spirit but the body as well.

Courage and Connection

Courage also enables us to satisfy our yearning for peace and human connection. We lawyers have this yearning like everyone else—it's just buried under our defenses. We enjoy the camaraderie of our peers, and the love of our families and significant others. We have soft spots for kids, pets, and underdogs. Yet, for most of our waking hours, we experience the opposite: combat. Our defenses make us combat-numb by the time we reach our mid-20's or soon thereafter. The numbness is reflected in the difficulty we have in other relationships and the way we shy away from anything that involves feelings as "too touchy-feely." I recall a psychologist once telling me that the healthier I became emotionally, the more difficult it would be to go to work. He meant that the more conscious I became of the pain of hostility, the harder it would be to face. I certainly found that to be true for many years. But I find the hostility more tolerable now for two reasons. First, because I provoke it much less often, less of it rebounds on me. Second, when hostility does come my way, I've gotten better at recognizing it for what it is—behavior based on fear. That realization makes it easier for me not to take it personally. However, I do confess that dealing with hostility, no matter how strong my defenses, is draining. Sadly for all of us, we are caught in a system that can relentlessly suffocate the spirit of peace and human connection.

In workshops for lawyers, where I often discuss the difference between competitive and cooperative game assumptions, I'll ask them, "According to which game assumption do you think other lawyers play?" Most lawyers answer, in effect, "The competitive one." I then ask, "If you could count on the other lawyer to play by the same assumption that you would choose, according to which assumption would you rather play?" The overwhelming majority say, "The cooperative one." This choice reflects an unrequited yearning for peace, for community. Older lawyers had another name for it: collegiality.

Courage enables us to risk moving closer to another long enough to unlock this yearning. Consider this letter I wrote to the opposing lawyer[41] to whom I lied about the availability of a witness (see Chapter 1):

Dear Terry:
This is one of those out-of-the-blue letters that may cause you to wonder what prompted it. To answer that question would involve telling you a story that would unduly prevail on your valuable time.
The purpose of this letter is that I want to acknowledge that I was unprofessional and dishonest in connection with my representation of my clients in a case that we tried together back in the

---

[41] I have used this lawyer's real name with his gracious permission.

early '80s. I was overly aggressive and discourteous, and I blatantly lied at least once that I remember. At the time, I rationalized all of the above on the theory that getting what I perceived to be a fair result for my clients justified the means that I chose.

I appreciate your indulging me this mea culpa.

Here was his eloquent response:

Dear Mark:

I'm having this letter typed so that it can be read. Sometimes you can read my writing but not reliably after it has grown cold.

I must confess that I had some lingering rancor as a result of the trial, but I hadn't thought about it in a good while. Thus, I was surprised to remember and feel it return to me when I saw your letter. I find it difficult to look back in my life and face some of the mean, cruel and common things that I have done, and I often cannot find any justification for them and wonder if I rationalized the justification, even at the time. I suppose what I am saying is, that I understand your feelings that you may be having and that I have had them myself.

Your letter means a lot to me, and you have a clean slate with me. Your honesty and courage in writing the letter has lifted from me the burden of my own anger, which I should have given up years ago. I thank you for that and I appreciate your letter very much.

/s/ J. Terry Weeks

Courage Preserves Relationships

Acting with courage preserves relationships. Not just during and after divorces, as we have seen, but in marriages, business relationships, and any human relationship, the courage to reach for community is what makes the relationship survive.

When we are in pseudo-community and chaos, we treat others as objects. In pseudo-community, we see the other person merely as a means to meet our needs. In chaos, we see the other person simply as an obstacle to having our needs met. When we have the courage to find emptiness, we eliminate our barriers to seeing others as having value independent of what they can do for us. We become able to follow the advice of Emanuel Kant, who said, "Always treat humanity as an end also and never only as a means" (Buber 16).

The courage to reach emptiness not only allows us to preserve relationships, but makes the relationships worth preserving. In chaos, we are most likely to experience others as "jerks"—or something considerably more profane. I used to think that a significant percentage of my profession—and certainly the majority of lawyers in Dallas, New York, and Chicago—were in fact odious body parts. I found that much of my time was spent in fear, fighting with them and being stressed by them.

During the process of emptiness, I realized the one commonality among all those odious body parts was that every time I saw one, I WAS THERE.[42] And so my corollary to Will Rogers' famous aphorism is, "*I have never met a jerk I didn't* make." I mean this in two ways. First, for someone to be a jerk, I have to judge him or her as such, and I am now rarely so arrogant. Second, I find that in emptiness, my own demeanor can powerfully influence those around me. People do not often relate to me as jerks because when I am in emptiness, I bring out the best in them.

I cannot imagine a profession that, day in and day out, gives a person more opportunities to be an odious body part than the legal profession. Moreover, as I have confessed, I have availed myself of those opportunities on many occasions. In recent years, however, I don't seem to run across that many jerks. The lawyers I encounter are basically ethical, civil, and responsible. They struggle against great adversity, including fear, to do the right thing. I do my best to bring out the basic goodness in them, and I have found that there is plenty there.

---

[42] This revelation came to me in a series of workshops, sponsored by Landmark Education, entitled "The Curriculum for Living."

A Simple Choice

Duality pervades our existence. Consider how many things are known chiefly in relation to their opposite: life/death, yin/yang, white/black, hot/cold, wet/dry, on/off. This same duality pervades our relationships. Some behaviors bring us closer to one another; others distance us. Behaviors that distance us come from a place of fear; behaviors that bring us together come from a place of courage.

In every interaction we have with other human beings, whether in our business or our personal relationships, we have a choice. One option is to approach the other person with fingers crossed and jaws clenched. We can wield the bludgeons of hostility until we gasp for breath. We can absorb the blows until we can no longer bear the pain.

Our other option is to summon the courage to approach the other person with an open heart. We can look into their eyes and *create* a mirror of the humanity within ourselves. With strength and without embarrassment we can seek to enliven the spirits of others. We can choose to experience that deep, warm and open feeling within our chests that tells us that we have made a human connection.

EPILOGUE

My greatest challenge and the source of my greatest reward as a lawyer and human being is the struggle to act on courage rather than fear. It requires consciousness of whether I am acting in integrity, consciousness of emotions, and consciousness of my relationships with myself and others, and whether I am in tune with the order of the universe. Moreover, taking responsibility for my part in unproductive conflict has required accepting and even loving those "ugly" parts of myself with which I am now familiar. Although none of this is or has been easy, it would be impossible without some tools.

In addition to the many insights that I have gained from the readings contained in the bibliography, I have learned much about myself and others through the process of individual and group psychotherapy. Through it, I began the process of self-discovery and acceptance. I have also learned much about the phases of human relationship through workshops conducted by the Foundation for Community Encouragement, P.O. Box 17210, Seattle, WA 98107; telephone (888) 784-9001. Through these powerful events, one can experience the deeply satisfying phase of community and learn the process of achieving it in one's everyday life. In addition, a recent study found that the workshops enabled participants to live more authentically and to better connect with others.

An organization called Landmark Education— 353 Sacramento Street, Suite 200, San Francisco, CA 94111; telephone (415) 882-6300—sponsors several courses designed to improve the quality of life of its participants. I gained some very useful insights about taking responsibility and also about the nature and power of integrity and leadership in Landmark's courses.

These organizations are by no means the exclusive ways to develop consciousness and maintain one's courage. Throughout the United States, there are literally thousands of providers of experiential learning, an essential tool for effective conflict resolution. For information, write Institute for Centered Conflict Resolution, 98 San Jacinto Boulevard, 600 San Jacinto Center, Austin, Texas 78701. The Institute develops courses specifically for lawyers and others interested in better ways to deal with conflict, and has information on other experiential learning opportunities.

APPENDIX A

THE TEXAS LAWYERS CREED —
A MANDATE FOR PROFESSIONALISM

I am a lawyer; I am entrusted by the People of Texas to preserve and improve our legal system. I am licensed by the Supreme Court of Texas. I must therefore abide by the Texas Disciplinary Rules of Professional Conduct, but I know that Professionalism requires more than merely avoiding the violation of laws and rules. I am committed to this Creed for no other reason than it is right.

I. OUR LEGAL SYSTEM

A lawyer owes to the administration of justice personal dignity, integrity, and independence. A lawyer should always adhere to the highest principles of professionalism.

1. I am passionately proud of my profession. Therefore, "My word is my bond."
2. I am responsible to assure that all persons have access to competent representation regardless of wealth or position in life.
3. I commit myself to an adequate and effective pro bono program.
4. I am obligated to educate my clients, the public, and other lawyers regarding the spirit and letter of this Creed.
5. I will always be conscious of my duty to the judicial system.

II. LAWYER TO CLIENT

A lawyer owes to a client allegiance, learning, skill, and industry. A lawyer shall employ all appropriate means to protect and advance the client's legitimate rights, claims, and objectives. A lawyer shall not be deterred by any real or imagined fear of judicial disfavor or public unpopularity, nor be influenced by mere self-interest.

1. I will advise my client of the contents of this Creed when undertaking representation.
2. I will endeavor to achieve my client's lawful objectives in legal transactions and in litigation as quickly and economically as possible.
3. I will be loyal and committed to my client's lawful objectives, but I will not permit that loyalty and commitment to interfere with my duty to provide objective and independent advice.

4. I will advise my client that civility and courtesy are expected and are not a sign of weakness.
5. I will advise my client of proper and expected behavior.
6. I will treat adverse parties and witnesses with fairness and due consideration. A client has no right to demand that I abuse anyone or indulge in any offensive conduct.
7. I will advise my client that we will not pursue conduct which is intended primarily to harass or drain the financial resources of the opposing party.
8. I will advise my client that we will not pursue tactics which are intended primarily for delay.
9. I will advise my client that we will not pursue any course of action which is without merit.
10. I will advise my client that I reserve the right to determine whether to grant accommodations to opposing counsel in all matters that do not adversely affect my client's lawful objectives. A client has no right to instruct me to refuse reasonable requests made by other counsel.
11. I will advise my client regarding the availability of mediation, arbitration, and other alternative methods of resolving and settling disputes.

III. LAWYER TO LAWYER

A lawyer owes to opposing counsel, in the conduct of legal transactions and the pursuit of litigation, courtesy, candor, cooperation, and scrupulous observance of all agreements and mutual understandings. Ill feelings between clients shall not influence a lawyer's conduct, attitude, or demeanor toward opposing counsel. A lawyer shall not engage in unprofessional conduct in retaliation against other unprofessional conduct.

1. I will be courteous, civil, and prompt in oral and written communications.
2. I will not quarrel over matters of form or style, but I will concentrate on matters of substance.
3. I will identify for other counsel or parties all changes I have made in documents submitted for review.
4. I will attempt to prepare documents which correctly reflect the agreement of the parties. I will not include provisions which have not been agreed upon or omit provisions which are necessary to reflect the agreement of the parties.
5. I will notify opposing counsel, and, if appropriate, the Court or other persons, as soon as practicable, when hearings, depositions, meetings, conferences or closings are cancelled.
6. I will agree to reasonable requests for extensions of time and for waiver of procedural formalities, provided legitimate objectives of my client will not be adversely affected.

7. I will not serve motions or pleadings in any manner that unfairly limits another party's opportunity to respond.
8. I will attempt to resolve by agreement my objections to matters contained in pleadings and discovery requests and responses.
9. I can disagree without being disagreeable. I recognize that effective representation does not require antagonistic or obnoxious behavior. I will neither encourage nor knowingly permit my client or anyone under my control to do anything which would be unethical or improper if done by me.
10. I will not, without good cause, attribute bad motives or unethical conduct to opposing counsel nor bring the profession into disrepute by unfounded accusations of impropriety. I will avoid disparaging personal remarks or acrimony towards opposing counsel, parties and witnesses. I will not be influenced by any ill feeling between clients. I will abstain from any allusion to personal peculiarities or idiosyncrasies of opposing counsel.
11. I will not take advantage, by causing any default or dismissal to be rendered, when I know the identity of an opposing counsel, without first inquiring about that counsel's intention to proceed.
12. I will promptly submit orders to the Court. I will deliver copies to opposing counsel before or contemporaneously with submission to the court. I will promptly approve the form of orders which accurately reflect the substance of the rulings of the Court.
13. I will not attempt to gain an unfair advantage by sending the Court or its staff correspondence or copies of correspondence.
14. I will not arbitrarily schedule a deposition, Court appearance, or hearing until a good faith effort has been made to schedule it by agreement.
15. I will readily stipulate to undisputed facts in order to avoid needless costs or inconvenience for any party.
16. I will refrain from excessive and abusive discovery.
17. I will comply with all reasonable discovery requests. I will not resist discovery requests which are not objectionable. I will not make objections nor give instructions to a witness for the purpose of delaying or obstructing the discovery process. I will encourage witnesses to respond to all deposition questions which are reasonably understandable. I will neither encourage nor permit my witness to quibble about words where their meaning is reasonably clear.
18. I will not seek Court intervention to obtain discovery which is clearly improper and not discoverable.
19. I will not seek sanctions or disqualification unless it is necessary for protection of my client's lawful objectives or is fully justified by the circumstances.

IV. LAWYER AND JUDGE

Lawyers and judges owe each other respect, diligence, candor, punctuality, and protection against unjust and improper criticism and attack. Lawyers and judges are equally responsible to protect the dignity and independence of the Court and the profession.

1. I will always recognize that the position of judge is the symbol of both the judicial system and administration of justice. I will refrain from conduct that degrades this symbol.
2. I will conduct myself in court in a professional manner and demonstrate my respect for the Court and the law.
3. I will treat counsel, opposing parties, the Court, and members of the Court staff with courtesy and civility.
4. I will be punctual.
5. I will not engage in any conduct which offends the dignity and decorum of proceedings.
6. I will not knowingly misrepresent, mischaracterize, misquote or miscite facts or authorities to gain an advantage.
7. I will respect the rulings of the Court.
8. I will give the issues in controversy deliberate, impartial, and studied analysis and consideration.
9. I will be considerate of the time constraints and pressures imposed upon the Court, Court staff and counsel in efforts to administer justice and resolve disputes.

APPENDIX B

PERLMUTTER & REAGAN, L.L.P. CLIENT SURVEY

1. To what extent were you satisfied with the results obtained for you by Perlmutter & Reagan, L.L.P.? **(Did you feel like you were better off because you hired us?)** *(Please rate on a scale of 1-5 with "5" meaning "very satisfied" and "1" meaning "very dissatisfied.")*

5   4   3   2   1

If you gave a rating of three or below to the above question, please elaborate.

2. To what extent were you satisfied that the cost of the services provided by Perlmutter & Reagan, L.L.P. was reasonable in relation to the value you received? **(Did you feel like you got your money's worth?)** *(Please rate on a scale of 1-5 with "5" meaning "very satisfied," "3" meaning "average" and "1" meaning "very dissatisfied.")*

5   4   3   2   1

If you gave a rating of three or below to the above question, please elaborate.

3. To what extent were you satisfied with your contact with the attorneys? **(Were they accessible, attentive and considerate?)** *(Please rate on a scale of 1-5 with "5" meaning "very satisfied" and "1" meaning "very dissatisfied.")*

5   4   3   2   1

If you gave a rating of three or below to the above question, please elaborate.

4. To what degree were you satisfied with your contact with the legal assistants and staff? (**Did you get the help you needed?**) *(Please rate on a scale of 1-5 with "5" meaning "very satisfied" and "1" meaning "very dissatisfied.")*

5   4   3   2   1

If you gave a rating of three or below to the above question, please elaborate.

5. How willing would you be to recommend Perlmutter & Reagan, L.L.P. in the future. (**Would you recommend us to your friends?**) *(Please rate on a scale of 1-5 with "5" meaning "very willing," "3" meaning "probably" and "1" meaning "totally unwilling.")*

5   4   3   2   1

If you gave a rating of three or below to the above question, please elaborate.

6. Please provide any additional thoughts on how we can better serve you.

Your Name (optional):

Telephone Number (optional):

Dear _____,

I want to take responsibility for what I have done to bring our relationship to where it is today. Although, even now, I may not be aware of all I have done to hurt you or to push you away, I want to tell you what I do know. Specifically....

I hope that what we are about to do will bring us closer together rather than drive us further apart. To that end, I pledge to do my best to be as respectful of your needs and feelings as my own, throughout the process. If you believe I am failing to do that, I would like you to remind me of my pledge.

Dear _____,

This letter is to acknowledge responsibility for my [organization's] part in bringing our business relationship to where it is today. Although, even now, I may not be aware of all that I [we] have done to contribute to our current situation, I do understand that these actions have caused difficulties: [identity specific conduct].

I am committed to finding a way to make amends for any problems that we have caused. Further, I pledge to you that we will work diligently toward a mutually satisfactory solution.

WORKS CITED

American Bar Association, Center for Professional Responsibility. *Model Rules of Professional Conduct*. Chicago: American Bar Association, 1995.

Bachman, Walt. *Law v. Life*. Rhinebeck: Four Directions, 1995.

Bok, Sisela. *Lying*. New York: Vintage, 1989.

Buber, Martin. *I and Thou*. Trans. Walter Kaufmann. New York: Scribner's, 1970.

"Cabbage Patch 'Attack' Prompts Suit." *Austin American-Statesman*. 11 Jan. 1997: A9.

Carville, James. *We're Right and They're Wrong*. New York: Random House, 1996.

Conger, Jay A., et al. *Spirit at Work: Discovering the Spirituality in Leadership*. New York: Jossey-Bass, 1994.

Covey, Stephen R. *The Seven Habits of Highly Effective People, Powerful Lessons in Personal Change*. New York: Fireside Simon & Schuster, 1989.

Crum, Thomas F. *The Magic of Conflict*. New York: Simon and Schuster, 1987.

Dorland's Illustrated Medical Dictionary. Philadelphia: Saunders, 1988.

Edelman, Lester. Comments from a meeting of the Dispute Avoidance Resource Task Force. Denver, 8 Mar. 1996.

Eichenwald, Kurt. "On Tape, Texaco Officials Plot to Shred Evidence in Bias Suit." *Austin American Statesman*, Monday, 4 Nov. 1996: 1+.

Evans, Richard. *Psychology and Arthur Miller*. New York: Dutton, 1969.

"Exhaustion, Psychological Stressors in the Work Environment, and Acute Myocardial Infarction in Adult Men." *Journal of Psychosomatic Research*. 36.8 (1992): 777-785.

Fox, Matthew. *The REinvention of Work: A New Vision of Livelihood for Our Time*. San Francisco: Harper, 1994.

Franken, Al. *Rush Limbaugh is a Big Fat Idiot and Other Observations*. New York: Dell, 1996.

Friedman, Meyer, M.D. and Ray H. Rosenman, M.D. *Type A Behavior and Your Heart*. New York: Knopf, 1974.

Gallagher, James L. Speech given in conjunction with "Strategic Overview of the Personal Injury Case—Defense." State Bar of Texas Advanced Personal Injury Course. Austin, 12 Jul. 1996.

Goleman, Daniel. *Emotional Intelligence, Why it can matter more than IQ*. New York: Bantam, 1995.

Gozdz, Kazimierz, ed. *Community Building, Renewing Spirit & Learning in Business*. San Francisco: New Leaders Sterling & Stone, 1995.

Graziano, William G., Lauri A. Jensen-Campbell, and Elizabeth C. Hair. "Perceiving Interpersonal Conflict and Reacting to It: The Case for Agreeableness." *Journal of Personality and Social Psychology* 70.4 (1966): 820-833.

Heschel, Abraham Joshua. *The Sabbath*. New York: Noonday, 1951.

Hirsch, Ellen, ed. *Facts About Israel*. Jerusalem: Israel Information Center, 1992.

Josephson, Michael. *Ethical Values, Attitudes, and Behaviors in American Schools*. Marina del Rey: Josephson Institute of Ethics, 1992.

Kaplan, Mordechai. *Questions Jews Ask*. New York: Reconstructionist, 1956, rev. 1966.

Kennedy, John F. *Profiles in Courage*. Memorial ed. New York: Harper & Row, 1964.

Kushner, Lawrence. *God Was In this Place and I, i Did Not Know*. Woodstock: Jewish Lights, 1991.

Lang, H. Jack, ed. *The Wit and Wisdom of Abraham Lincoln As Reflected in His Briefer Letters and Speeches*. Cleveland: World, 1941.

Mitchell, Stephen. *Tao Te Ching*. New York: Harper Perennial—Harper Collins, 1991.

Mixon, John and Gordon Otto. *Continuous Quality Improvement, Law, and Legal Education*. Emory Law Journal 43 (1994): 393-505.

"National Criminal Justice Measures Affecting State Courts." *Caseload Highlights, Examining the Work of The State Courts* 2.1 (1966): 1+.

Osterberg, Rolf. *Corporate Renaissance*. Mill Valley: Nataraj, 1993.

Papantonio, Mike. *In Search of Atticus Finch, A Motivational Book for Lawyers*. Pensacola: Seville, 1995.

Patterson, James and Peter Kim. *The Day America Told the Truth*. New York: Prentice Hall, 1991.

Peck, M. Scott. *The Different Drum*. New York: Touchstone, 1987.

The Pentateuch and Haftorahs. Ed. J.H. Hertz. New York: Soncino, 1960.

Ralston, Peter. *Cheng Hsin: The Principles of Effortless Power*. Berkeley: North Atlantic, 1989.

Rioch, Margaret J. "The Work of Wilfred Bion on Groups." *Psychiatry*. 33.1 (1970): 56-66.

Sells, Benjamin. *The Soul of the Law*. Rockport: Element, 1994.

"Separating the Just from the Jerks." *U.S. Business Litigation*. 2.6 (1997): 24-29.

Solzhenitsyn, Aleksandr Isaevich. *The Gulag Archipelago*. Trans. Thomas P. Whitney. New York: Harper Perennial, 1991.

Spivey, Broadus A. "Strategic Overview of the Personal Injury Case—Plaintiff." Speech given in conjunction with State Bar of Texas Advanced Personal Injury Course, Austin, 12 Jul. 1996.

TEXAS DISCIPLINARY RULES OF PROFESSIONAL CONDUCT, *reprinted in* TEX. GOV'T CODE ANN., tit. 2, subtit. G. app. (Vernon 1988 and Supp. 1997).

Texas Tech Law Review 27.3 (1996).

"Uncivil Suit." *The Texas Lawyer*. 17 Jun., 1996: 3.

"Value For Litigation Dollar a Slippery Concept." *U.S. Business Litigation* 1.1 (Spring 1996): 1+.

Watts, Alan. *Tao, The Watercourse Way*. New York: Pantheon, 1975.

Weinberg, Steve. "Hardball Discovery." *ABA Journal* Nov. 1995: 66+.

Wheatley, Margaret. *Leadership and the New Science*. San Francisco: Berrett-Koehler, 1992.

"When You Need a Lawyer." *Consumer Reports*. Feb. 1996: 34-39.

White, Stephen W. Rev. of *The Litigation Explosion: What Happened When America Unleashed the Lawsuit?*, by Walter K. Olson. *The Annals of the American Academy of Political and Social Sciences* 520 (Mar. 1992): 203-204.

Williamson, Marianne. *A Return to Love*. New York: Harper Paperbacks—Harper Collins, 1994.

"Woman, 11-Year Old Return Money from Brinks Crash." *Austin American-Statesman*. 11 Jan. 1997: A9.

Zimbardo, Phillip. "The Psychology of Evil: On the Perversion of Human Potential." *Advances in the Study of Communication and Affect*. Vol. 4. New York: Plenum, 1978.

INDEX

NOTES

NOTES

NOTES

NOTES